BEYOND THE ZOOM:
THE AFTERLIFE

BEYOND THE ZOOM:
THE AFTERLIFE

George Augustus Stallings, Jr.

SKS PRESS
Washington, D.C.

Production and creative:
jonathangullery.design@gmail.com
Cover photo by Amir Esrafili on Unsplash

FIRST EDITION

ISBN Paperback: 978-0-9745586-1-5
ISBN Cloth: 978-0-9745586-2-2
ISBN Ebook: 978-0-9745586-3-9

Printed in the United States of America

To our Ancestors, who have returned unto the Source
from whence they came.
May God, our Heavenly Parent,
who "is merciful and gracious, slow to anger,
and plenteous in mercy" (Ps. 108:8/KJV)
forgive their sins
as they repent of their transgressions.
May they live IN God
as they await us to join them in that state
of perfect peace and eternal bliss.

CONTENTS

LIST OF ABBREVIATIONS

Bible Translations (referenced in this book)

AMP	Amplified Bible
ESV	English Standard Version
ISV	International Standard Version
KJV	King James Version
NAB	New American Bible
NAS	New American Standard
NASB	New American Standard Bible
NIV	New International Version
NKJV	New King James Version
NLT	New Living Translation
NRS	New Revised Standard
RSV	Revised Standard Version

Books of the Bible (referenced in this book)

Gen.	Genesis
Exod.	Exodus
Deut.	Deuteronomy
Ps.	Psalms
Prov.	Proverbs
Eccles.	Ecclesiastes
Ws	Wisdom
Sir.	Sirach
Isa.	Isaiah
Jer.	Jeremiah
Ezek.	Ezekiel
Mic.	Micah
Matt.	Matthew
Mark	Mark
Luke	Luke
Rom.	Romans
1 Cor.	1 Corinthians
2 Cor.	2 Corinthians
Gal.	Galatians
Eph.	Ephesians
Phil.	Philippians
Col.	Colossians
1 Thess.	1 Thessalonians
2 Tim.	2 Timothy
Heb.	Hebrews
1 Pet.	1 Peter
2 Pet.	2 Peter
Rev.	Revelation

The Usage of Pronouns When Referring to God

In referring to God in the pronoun form, the masculine reference is used in this book, since most persons are accustomed to viewing God in that context. However, according to the Bible, "God is Spirit" (John 4:24/ NAB). While God is referenced traditionally as masculine, Spirit is genderless. Therefore, one can properly use the terminology Mother/Father God and remain biblically faithful, since God embodies both masculine and feminine qualities as the Supreme Parent of all humankind. Indeed, it is recorded in the Book of Genesis 1:27 (NAB) that "God created mankind in his image; in the image of God he created them; male and female he created them."

Preface

Namaste!

"The God in Me recognizes and greets the presence of the God in You!" In that single Hindu expression lies the essence of life, love, and lineage. It provides the pathway to discovering and understanding that which makes us "live and move and have our being" (Acts 17:28). What is it? It is the eternal presence of the invisible God dwelling within mortal flesh. It is the very Essence of God, breathed into a corporeal mass as a supreme act of love at the moment of human conception in a woman's womb (Gen. 2:7) that gives to every person created in the image and likeness of God (Gen. 1:26) the life that resides solely in God and, by thus doing so, conveys God's lineage from one person to another, from one generation to the next.

It was God's original intention that man and woman would be the visible and tangible manifestation of the invisible God on Earth (Gen. 1:26), offering their "earthen vessels" (2 Cor. 2:7/NAB), that is, their bodies formed from the dust (Gen. 2:7), as the dwelling place of God, who is Spirit (John 4:24). Such a feat could be achieved and accomplished only if they obeyed God's Word by accepting their portion of responsibility to be "fruitful, multiply, and take dominion over the earth" (Gen. 1:28). Created to be the "mirrors" of God, reflecting God's image and likeness in substantial form, God bestowed upon man and woman the divine traits, characteristics, and attributes that reside within the Godhead. Thus, a plainspoken biblical truth is that God's ultimate desire is for man and woman to become the visible God on Earth!

Through a process of achieving individual spiritual maturity, man could find his mate and woman her man and the two of them become one body (Gen. 2:24), reflecting the Oneness of God in visible form. Together, they would multiply, fill the Earth, bring it into submission, and take dominion over it (Gen. 1:28). Thus, God created them as spirit beings robed in flesh to be the "home" where God would dwell and function on the Earth. The Scriptures speak directly to this belief: "Do you not know that you are the temple of God, and that the Spirit of God dwells in you? If anyone destroys God's temple, God will destroy that person, for the temple of God, which you are, is holy" (1 Cor. 3:16–17/NAB).

This is reiterated and reinforced in the same book in another chapter: "Do you not know that your body is a temple of the holy Spirit within you, whom you have from God, and that you are not your own?" (1 Cor. 6:19/ NAB).

The very Essence of the unseen God residing and moving in man and woman is God's eternal gift to humanity. In 2 Corinthians 4:7, we read, "But we hold this treasure in earthen vessels, that the surpassing power may be of God and not from us." Our very being belongs to God. Yes, you and I are God's property, for we "have been purchased at a price" (1 Cor. 6:20/ NAB).

In faith, we believe that the life we possess does not solely belong to us, but is the Essence of the Spirit of God, called *ruach* in Hebrew, *pneuma* in Greek, and *wind* or *breath* in English, residing in us. The Word of God highlights this concept, as found in the letter of the apostle Paul to the Romans

(14:7–9/NAB): "None of us lives for oneself, and no one dies for oneself. For if we live, we live for the Lord, and if we die, we die for the Lord; so then, whether we live or die, we are the Lord's." It is comforting and reassuring to hear, believe, and embrace those words. It reminds us that what ultimately will prevail is the very essence of life itself: spirit. Not even physical death can deprive us of life, because death does not own life. Life belongs of God and to those upon whom God freely bestows it as a visible and tangible expression of Self. In every moment, God, as Creator and Heavenly Parent, is constantly sending forth life from Himself while simultaneously receiving life back unto Himself once it has run its course in the flesh. In physical death, life is changed, not ended!

Beyond the Zoom: The Afterlife will challenge many of the core concepts and notions of faith that you have cherished since you were a child and as you moved from adolescence to adulthood. The traditional notion of Heaven and what it consists of is one of those cherished beliefs. So much of our understanding of life after death has been shaped and molded by catechesis and preaching that is not accurately aligned or refined through the prism of Scripture but consists of a compilation of myths and fairy tales mixed with a few biblical references that have portrayed a false notion of where the spirit goes after leaving the body.

The content of the pages within *Beyond the Zoom: The Afterlife* is not an attempt to tamper with, destroy, debunk, or confuse readers in regard to their cherished "BS" (belief system) but a humble attempt to simply offer an alternative viewpoint of life after death that is more biblically aligned, by "connecting the dots" of what the Word of God actually says about the things that we cherish the most in regard to life after death.

At times, you will question or even reject what is presented. As Yeshua Hamashiach (Jesus the Christ) said, "Let not your hearts be troubled;

believe in God, believe also in me" (John 14:1/RSV). It all boils down to belief. We should dispense with the conservative attitude of faith, which makes us afraid to question conventional beliefs and traditional doctrines that we may have neither researched nor fully understood.

Whether or not you believe what you read within these pages will depend on where you are in your personal journey of faith. No one can tell you what or how to believe. It rests in your hands. Take it to God in prayer, and you will find the answers that will bring you to a greater understanding of what God has in store for those who love God and believe in God's Word.

A note on the methodology employed in the composition of this book:

Whenever one is attempting to expose another person to a new concept that can radically shape, affect, or alter his or her way of thinking and believing, it takes more than hearing it once. It must be reiterated continuously until it reaches the point of saturation — in this case positive indoctrination. Oftentimes, there needs to be a deprogramming of one's previous beliefs before a reprogramming of new concepts and ideas can be deposited in and embraced by the believer. Every effort has been made within the pages of this book to reference and re-reference biblical passages and "buzz phrases" that undergird the spiritual principles outlined. Certain references will be often repeated, as "dots are connected" from different angles and perspectives.

There is also another deep concern: If the reader skips a particular chapter or "jumps" to chapters that seem more interesting, without reading the entire book, he may be less able to capture the premises that build up to the conclusion of the book's thesis. In some instances, repetition can be a productive tool in creating a "layering effect" in establishing and solidifying a new approach when viewing death and the Afterlife from a new paradigm. Overall, each chapter possibly can stand on its own in giving the reader a bird's-eye view of an approach to the Afterlife that is more biblically connected.

Finally, the book is short, not long, because life is short and there is no time for lollygagging! The remainder of our time on Earth needs to be focused on preparing for the "Great Release," the "Great Return," and the "Welcome Home," rather than being immersed in reading an elongated treatise with no change in thought or action occurring. The major task that lies before the reader is comprehending the new paradigm shift and incarnating it in his or her daily thoughts and living.

May you greet and recognize the presence of God that dwells within you as you seek to become the visible and tangible manifestation of God on Earth! After all, it is your purpose for having been born and your divine destiny to return unto God when this world can afford you a home no longer in the flesh.

After reading the book, it will be your decision as a believer to decide what "BS" best aligns with your core beliefs about life after death. You can be instructed or guided in a particular way or path, but in the final analysis, the decision rests solely with you!

Let not your heart be troubled!

NAMASTE!

IN GRATITUDE

I am eternally grateful to those who played an indispensable role in bringing this manuscript to fruition in book form. My heart shall always rejoice and be exceedingly glad for each of you.

For all of the hard work, assistance, and heavy doses of encouragement I received at every step in the research and compilation of material that led to the publication of this book, I feel a deep sense of gratitude to:

God, My Heavenly Parent and Eternal Lover of my soul. I give You thanks and praise for having so fearfully and wonderfully made me and imparted to me wisdom, knowledge, and understanding.

Dorothy Smith Stallings, my beloved Mom, most loyal and devoted friend, and greatest critic whose undying love, consistent encouragement, and endless motherly prayers provided the strength I needed to go the distance in completing this challenging project.

Jonathan Gullery, who designed, formatted, and shepherded the book to the finish line.

Robert "Bob" Selle who performed a yeoman's job as chief copy editor, critic, and reviewer.

Bishop Diane Adiah Peters, who read every chapter of the original manuscript and offered invaluable constructive feedback.

The clergy, lay leadership, and parishioners of Imani Temple African American Catholic Congregation worldwide. Their faithful stewardship and prayerful support helped me to accomplish what seemingly was an impossible task. I love them with a shepherd's heart.

Your word is a lamp to guide my feet
and a light for my path.
— Ps. 119:105/NLT

Let's Face It, Not Fear It!

Let's face it: We are all going to die, no exceptions allowed! So we may as well get over it! While we may have limited control over the circumstances or situation involving our eventual demise, we cannot prevent or escape it. As painful a thought as it may be, our attitude or disposition toward our own death contributes greatly to our ability to see life as it is and to live it more abundantly.

I am often given to a reflection of my own personal death. For some reason, I simply cannot imagine what it must be like to be dead! Even though I have presided over hundreds of funerals and witnessed the deceased lying in state, it appalls me when thinking about others eventually gawking over my mortal remains and trying to guesstimate what ordeal led to my demise. How macabre!

What causes people to fear death? I think it has less to do with death itself and more with the HOW, WHEN, WHAT, and WHERE of death. How will I die? When or at what stage will it occur? What will be the cause of my death? Will it be natural, accidental, via a terminal illness? Will I die in the prime of my life or at a ripe old age? Where will I be when it happens: at home, on travel, on a highway or train, in midflight, on takeoff or landing, in a river, ocean, or lake while swimming, as a result of a murder, on the way from work or home, et cetera? Yet we know that death is not a respecter of any of these circumstances.

Even though we know that death will come to each of us, none of us knows the exact time or hour of its visitation. Death strikes when and where it will!

Since physical death is inevitable, what adjustments must be made to prepare for it? First, we must come to a recognition and acceptance of the limitations of our finiteness. We were not born in the flesh to dwell in it forever. If you are a believer in the Word of God, you can find comfort and consolation in God's promise found in 2 Corinthians 5: 1–8 (NIV):

> For we know that if the earthly tent we live in is destroyed, we have a building from God, an eternal house in heaven, not built by human hands. Meanwhile, we groan, longing to be clothed instead with our heavenly dwelling, because when we are clothed, we will not be found naked. For while we are in this tent, we groan and are burdened, because we do not wish to be unclothed but to be clothed instead with our heavenly dwelling, so that what is mortal may be swallowed up by life. Now the one who has fashioned us for this very purpose is God, who has given us the Spirit as a deposit, guaranteeing what is to come.
>
> Therefore, we are always confident and know that as long as we are at home in the body we are away from the Lord. For we live by faith, not by sight. We are confident, I say, and would prefer to be away from the body and at home with the Lord.

It all boils down to believing that it will occur as the Word of God has stated, because it is not verifiable in FACT. There is nothing scientific or empirical about it. It is based solely on FAITH. If you believe that God is Sovereign and true to His Word, then you can be confident and rely on His promise that there is life after physical death, though in a way that the human mind cannot even begin to fathom.

But what kind of life or existence is it? Does one continue to exist with individual consciousness or self-awareness? Will the person *know* that he or she has left Earth and entered into some type of celestial realm? Will those who have preceded the deceased in death be met or recognized by the one who has passed? Will the deceased be one among zillions of others who have died, eternally living in a space or place that has no boundaries or physical constraints? As pure spirit, will the deceased function and operate in the same manner and proportions as the Eternal Spirit from whence they originally came? Will the deceased lose individual consciousness to the extent that they will retain no knowledge of their earthly existence, in the same way in which a person has no knowledge of prior existence before reaching human consciousness?

All of these questions beg for an answer, and the lack of response can cause a person to fear and tremble at the very thought of having to die or depart from this Earth.

But why worry about things over which you have little or no control? As the Spanish say: "Qué será, será!" or "What will be, will be!" Even the Book of Ecclesiastes reminds us that there is a time and season for every purpose under the heavens — a time to be born and a time to die (Eccles. 3:1–2/ NAB). As the ancients declared: "We live to die."

When I accept the reality of my own death, I no longer fear or own it. I let it go and let God have His way. I cannot keep what is not mine or that which is not my eternal destiny. Death is only a temporary eruption, a hiccup, if you will, that clears the pathway for the spirit's return unto the Source from whence it originally came (Eccles. 12:7). "Do not be afraid of those who kill the body but cannot kill the soul" (Matt. 10:28/NIV).

Let's face it, not fear it! Even though we are all going to die, death will not have the last word, and it will not be the final chapter of our lives. There is nothing to fear about death. In the words of the thirty-second president of the United States, Franklin Delano Roosevelt, "We have nothing to fear but fear itself." Those words can easily be applied to death itself. If you need spiritual reinforcement, call death by its name and say to it, "Where, O death, is your victory? Where, O death is your sting?" (1 Cor. 15:55/NIV).

CHAPTER 1

Let's Start at the Very Beginning

Maria, the protagonist in the classic film *The Sound of Music*, serenaded the children of the von Trapp family with the lyrics, "Let's start at the very beginning. A very good place to start." So, let us do just that!

For the believer, all human life begins with, is sustained by, and ends in God, the Creator of life itself. As people of faith, we believe that, apart from God's invisible Spirit dwelling in our mortal frame, we are as good as dead because there is no life or breath within us.

When God said, "Let Us make man in Our Image and Likeness" (Gen. 1:26), it pertained to the very Essence and nature of God, which is Pure Spirit. We read in the Gospel of John 4:24 that "God is Spirit, and those who worship God must worship in Spirit and truth" (NAB). If we are to understand that which makes man and woman live, move, and have their being (Acts 17:28), then we have to explore what is the Essence and nature of God who breathed us into existence — namely, what are the divine traits, characteristics, and attributes of God, which also reside in those created in the image and likeness of God?

The Divine Traits, Characteristics, and Attributes of God

"God is absolute," which means that God is a Pure Spirit, minus any imperfection. As a Supreme Being, God is perfect and complete within Himself and free from any restriction or limitation of any kind. There is no failure in God. God is resolute and just in all of His thoughts, ways, and actions. Man and woman are called and chosen by the invisible God to mirror Him on Earth. This can be achieved by reaching a level of spiritual maturity with a mind and heart of God that will place humans in a position to take dominion over all things that God has created.

"God is unique," which means that God has no equal, is unparalleled, and is incomparable. God exists as the Only One and the Sole Example of what man and woman should strive to become and achieve, namely, "little gods," reflecting the image and likeness of God. He did not make the birds of the air, the fish in the sea, or the cattle grazing on the hillside to mirror or resemble Himself. That has been reserved for man and woman alone. The uniqueness of God is manifested in each and every one of us. No two persons are exactly the same. We all possess a distinctive uniqueness because we are spiritual offspring of the one, true, unique God.

"God is unchanging," which means that God is not subject to the whims and notions of creation, not even to that of human beings. God is God all by Himself. God is the same in all of His Ways, possessing an unchanging nature that is our safety net and blessed assurance.

"God is spirit," which means that God is invisible. You cannot see or touch spirit, but you can feel its presence. As people of faith, we believe that God exists in spirit. In other words, just because God cannot be seen does not mean that He does not exist. An exercise I use often while conducting a funeral is asking the family and those in attendance to place their hand in front of their mouth and blow their breath into it (this exercise can be a bit challenging in the age of COVID when people may be wearing a mask). I then ask everyone, "Did you see it?" Of course, everyone responds with a resounding "NO." I follow up by saying: "But did you feel it?" And the response is, "YES!" The illustration is a simple demonstration to prove that you do not have to see something to believe it exists. God is invisible but takes on visibility by residing in man and woman (1 Cor. 3:16), created from the dust of the Earth, into which God blew "the breath of life" and made them living beings (Gen. 2:7).

"God is eternal," which means that God is "Alpha and Omega, the first and the last, with no beginning and no end." All times and seasons belong to God. Without God, human life would vanish in the twinkling of an eye. That which is eternal cannot die but can only be transformed. If you believe that God is eternal, then it follows that man and woman, the spiritual off-spring and seeds of God, would also bear the strain within their mortal flesh that is eternal and, therefore, possess something within their essence and nature that cannot die.

"God is omnipotent," which means that God is all-powerful. Nothing is beyond God's might, strength, or endurance. Man and woman possess the seeds of omnipotence. If allowed to germinate on the pathway to achieving spiritual maturity or perfection, they can accomplish the unimaginable and become more than conquerors because of the One who loves them (Rom. 8:37).

"God is omniscient," which means that God is completely aware and knows all things. Man and woman have the seeds of the same innate divine knowledge residing within them. Again, the requirement is striving for spiritual perfection, which is the supreme calling of every person created in the image and likeness of God. Jesus the Christ (Yeshua Hamashiach) underscored this attribute when he said, "So be perfect, just as your heavenly Father is perfect" (Matt. 5:48/NAB)."

"God is omnipresent," which means that God is present anywhere and everywhere at the same time. As a Spirit Entity, God is not limited by time and space. God's eternal presence defies any and all constrictions. There are no borders or restrictions to God's ability to be One in All in every circumstance and situation. Man and woman, possessing the eternal spirit of the Living God, will eventually reach the fullness of their Creator's omnipresence or ubiquitous nature once the spirit is released from the imprisoning confines of the body and returns to God to become one in God as God is One. As the renowned French theologian Pierre Teilhard de Chardin challenged humanity during his earthly life to "Release the imprisoned splendor within you," so will that splendor be completely released when we come into the fullness of God's omnipresence.

Once we understand the Essence and nature of God, the Creator, we are able to search the labyrinth of self to find our real identity, rightful purpose, and final destiny. Our focus is on striving and aspiring to be holy, righteous, and pure, as God Is the ultimate paradigm of holiness, righteousness, and purity. We seek to become so symmetrically aligned with God's will and plan for our lives that we can reflect the nature of the invisible God by performing the works that only God and those made in God's image and likeness can achieve.

Let the journey begin!

CHAPTER 2

The Afterlife in Mythology and World Religion

While the Afterlife cannot be scientifically or empirically proven as fact, it is, nonetheless, a part of the core belief systems of civilizations since time immemorial. It is enshrined in mythology as well as the traditions and teachings of practically every major religion in the world. Life is viewed as more than life in the flesh. It continues to exist and thrive in another extraterrestrial place or state of existence — that is, either in spirit form or through reincarnation. Regardless of what form life takes beyond the grave, it is believed that in death, life is changed, not ended.

No one knows with certainty the exactitude of a person's full nature after death. Even though there have been innumerable vivid accounts of persons with near-death experiences encountering bursts of pure light so powerfully overwhelming that it blinded the senses, they did not fully enter into that realm. No one who has physically died has returned to Earth to tell humanity exactly what the Otherworld consists of or who resides there.

The mystery of life after death is the greatest guarded secret of all time. It will only be revealed in its totality when we return unto the Source from whence we originally came. In that moment, we become AS or LIKE the One who created us (1 John 3:2).

The ancients possessed a wisdom that allowed them to have an innate sense of the mystery of life and death. After all, how could man and woman stand in a superior position in Creation, endowed with reason and infinite faculties, and not embrace a concept of life beyond the grave? As civilization developed and expanded, an oral tradition arose that passed on a view of the Afterlife from one generation to another. Later, it was synthesized into a systematic structure of belief.

The Afterlife, as viewed by mythology, predates any description of it in the formalized religions of the world. Such an understanding raises many questions as to the originality of the concept of life after death (or the life to come) found in the sacred texts of the various religions. Did religions draw from more predated nonbiblical sources of the Afterlife as the framework for contriving their own belief systems about life after death? Or does the universality of afterlife notions throughout human history validate the belief, whether nonbiblical or biblical, that there is something inherent in life that continues beyond the grave?

One source has the following to say about Otherworld beliefs:

> The afterlife (also referred to as life after death or the world to come) is a purported existence in which the essential part of an individual's identity or their stream of consciousness continues to live after the death of their physical body. According to various ideas about the afterlife, the essential aspect of the individual that lives on after death may be some partial element, or the entire soul or spirit, of an individual, which carries with it and may confer personal identity or, on the contrary, nirvana. Belief

in an afterlife is in contrast to the belief in oblivion after death ("Afterlife"/Wikipedia).

Views of the Afterlife in mythology and, later, contained within ancient religions range from souls continuing to live on at a higher level of activity (in a place called the *nether world*) to reincarnation, which allowed them to function in another form at a heightened (or diminished) level of consciousness.

Traditional African religions were diverse in their beliefs in an afterlife: "Hunter-gatherer societies such as the Hadza have no particular belief in an afterlife, and the death of an individual is a straightforward end to their existence" ("Afterlife"/Wikipedia). On the other hand,

> Ancestor cults are found throughout Sub-Saharan Africa, including cultures like the Yombe, Beng, Yoruba, and Ewe. [T]he belief that the dead come back into life and are reborn into their families is given concrete expression in the personal names that are given to children. … What is reincarnated are some of the dominant characteristics of the ancestor and not his soul. For each soul remains distinct, and each birth represents a new soul ("Afterlife"/Wikipedia).

Egyptian mythology contains numerous accounts of persons being buried alive with deceased Pharoahs in order for the slaves to continue serving and attending their earthly leaders in the Afterlife. Excavation of the burial grounds of these ancient rulers, most notably in the Pyramids, reveals that they contained food, clothing, and items used in everyday Egyptian life. In fact, the Pyramids were designed specifically as tombs to be the eternal dwelling places of kings, with all of the necessary accoutrements required to allow them to live luxuriously and eternally after physical death.

In Greek mythology, the underworld is an Otherworld where souls go after death:

> The original Greek idea of afterlife is that, at the moment of death, the soul is separated from the corpse, taking on the shape of the former person, and is transported to the entrance of the underworld. The underworld itself, referred to as Hades, is described as being either at the outer bounds of the ocean or beneath the depths or ends of the earth. It is considered the dark counterpart to the brightness of Mount Olympus, with the kingdom of the gods. The underworld is a realm invisible to the living, made solely for the dead ("Greek Underworld"/Wikipedia).

The Greeks believed in an afterlife or another world and that death was not a complete end to life or human existence. Such a belief became woven into their core religious practices and manifested itself in their burial rituals and practices.

As world religions developed and institutionalized over the course of time, they concretized beliefs similar to one another about the meaning of eternal life. Regardless of each sect's religious belief systems, when it came to the issue of life after death, religions shared a common thread that basically presented life after death as a change, not an end. They developed rituals and teachings to serve as sources and guides in preparing their adherents for eternal life. "Theists generally believe some afterlife awaits people when they die. Many religions, whether they believe in the soul's existence in another world, like Christianity, Islam, and many pagan belief systems, or reincarnation, like many forms of Hinduism and Buddhism, believe that one's status in the afterlife is a consequence of one's conduct during life" ("Afterlife"/Wikipedia).

The main Abrahamic faiths — Judaism, Christianity, and Islam — all embrace some form of an afterlife. Some sectors of Judaism even believe in reincarnation, while the Baha'i faith teaches that "the nature of the afterlife is beyond the understanding of those living, just as an unborn fetus cannot understand the nature of the world outside of the womb" ("Afterlife"/ Wikipedia).

In conclusion, whether a person draws his or her beliefs about the Afterlife from mythology, ancient religions, the religion of the Abrahamic faiths, or the religions of the East (such as Sufism, Buddhism, Hinduism, Jainism, Sikhism, Shinto, or traditional African religions), it can be said without hesitation that most of humanity believes in some form of life beyond the grave. Accordingly, it is a safe bet to anticipate some form of existence beyond this terrestrial plane, even if no one knows for certain exactly how it will unfold.

CHAPTER 3

Beyond the Zoom: The Afterlife

Our days may come to seventy years, or eighty, if our strength endures;
yet the best of them are but trouble and sorrow,
for they quickly pass, and we fly away. — Ps. 90:10/NIV

The *Zoom* refers to the short span of earthly life, in comparison to the Afterlife that begins after physical death. Life in the flesh is subjected to the Zoom Effect. It passes away quickly "in the moment, in the twinkling of an eye" (1 Cor. 15:52/KJV). Just when the band of life strikes up the beat and we get our groove on, it all seems to quickly come to an end like a flash in the pan! From the womb to the tomb, zoom! Zoom, zoom, zoom — and we are gone! Thus, it can be called the Zoom Effect!

Life, however, in the fullness of the spirit, is attuned only to its Creator. It is called the *Afterlife*. Death has no place where only the spirit dwells. Only that which God created can survive and thrive as a part of God's Essence. The deuterocanonical Book of Wisdom states:

Because God did not make death, nor does he rejoice in the destruction of the living. For he fashioned all things that they might have being; and the creatures of the world are wholesome, And there is not a destructive drug among them nor any domain of the nether world on earth (1:13–14/NAB).

For God formed man to be imperishable; the image of his own nature he made him. But by the envy of the devil, death entered the world, and they who are his possession experience it (2:23–24/ NAB).

If an individual does a comparative analysis between a human being's time in the flesh versus time from the viewpoint of God, the former is a minuscule form of existence measured against the latter. Man and woman view life chronologically (from the Greek word *chronos*), whereas God views all things from the vantage point of God's appointed time (the Greek word *kairos*). If the time of a person's mortal existence barely reaches a century, should not one's emphasis or focus be placed on life *after* physical death rather than being absorbed and preoccupied with physical life here on Earth? There is life after the "dash."

The Bible emphatically states that our physical presence on the Earth is but for a season. It also informs us that there is "a time to be born, and a time to die" (Eccles. 3:2). A thousand years in the sight of God are like a day that has just gone by, or like a watch in the night (Ps. 90:4). "So, our life will pass away like the traces of a cloud, and will be dispersed like a mist pursued by the sun's rays and overpowered by its heat. For our lifetime is the passing of a shadow; and our dying cannot be deferred, because it is fixed with a seal; and no one returns" (Ws 2:4b–5/NAB). What do these biblical passages reveal to us?

The Word of God reminds us that life in the flesh cannot last forever.

"Time is filled with swift transition, none on earth unmoved can stand," states the hymn. "Hold to God's Unchanging Hand. Build your hopes on things eternal, hold to God's Unchanging Hand." Life in the flesh is short-lived. Therefore, we should never live our lives in such a way that we think that all life is contained and summarized in this temporal or transitional state of existence.

"O God, Our Help in Ages Past", another great hymn of the Christian church, sums it up succinctly:

A thousand ages in Thy sight
Are like an evening gone
Short as the watch that ends the night
Before the rising sun.
Time, like an ever-rolling stream
Bears all its sons away.
They fly forgotten, as a dream
Dies at the opening day
Oh God, our help in ages past
Our hope for years to come
Be Thou our guide while troubles last
And our eternal home.

To live for a season, only to die? That's a wakeup call that doesn't bring much joy or "blessed assurance" to anyone who has everything to live for and nothing to die for! Yet, if we live long enough, we soon come to the realization that physical death is inevitable and there is no escaping it. Added to the fact that life is so fleeting, one could become quite disillusioned, depressed, and frustrated in trying to make the best of an ultimately dying situation.

How does one find wholeness and fulfillment in light of such a reality?

The answer lies in the depths of a person's faith or trust in God and self. In the Old Testament, the psalmist, described as King David, declares, "For You [Lord] will not abandon me to Sheol [the underworld], nor let your servant see the pit. You will show me the path to life, abounding joy in Your presence, the delights at Your right hand forever" (Ps. 16:10–11/ NAB).

Meditate and think about it for a moment: Why would God create us out of the Godhead just for a season only to allow us to be separated from the Source after we lie down in the sleep of death? After all, can God abandon Self?

For the believer, in death, life is changed, not ended. As propitious as it may sound, do you really believe it? Can you receive it? If so, it is yours! But, when the hour of death comes, it is not going to be a change that can be comprehended fully by human intelligence. For the thoughts of God are not our thoughts, and God's ways are not our ways (Isa. 55:8–9). God's thoughts and ways exceedingly surpass anything that the human mind could ever think or imagine. The real mystery of life and death lies in God. It will only be unraveled when each of us returns to the Source from whence we came and become One with It (Eccles. 12:7). Then, we shall know as God knows, for we shall be like or as God Is (1 John 3:2).

As the saying goes, "Everybody wants to go to Heaven, but nobody wants to die." How true it is! No matter how deep a person's faith and trust in God may be, there is a part of our humanity that is resistant to letting go of what we know, no matter how uncertain and temporary earthly life is for us. Change can be so difficult to handle and accept when we have no control over it, especially when it has to do with the greatest paradigm shift one could ever imagine: from Earth to eternity!

What happens to us if there is no life after death or we end up in a state of existence that we did not anticipate? The Book of Ecclesiastes even probes the question: "Who knows whether the spirit of man goes upward and the spirit of the beast goes down into the earth?" (3:3/ESV). Yet, on the other hand, the prophet Job confessed, "The spirit of the Lord has made me, and the breath of the Almighty gives me life" (32:8/ESV) and "As long as my breath is in me, and the spirit of God is in my nostrils" (27:3). Job believed in the depths of his soul that "breath" not only signified "life" but life that would continue on even after it left the body.

One thing is for certain: There is no way to slow down the clock or turn back the hands of time. While death is an occurrence of nature, life after death is supernatural and falls outside of the realm of verifiable truth. It all boils down to trust in God, as Creator, and a belief system that enshrines the mysteries of our faith and relationship with God.

When physical death comes for each of us, it is our time! In fact, there is no such thing as dying before one's time. For when death comes, that is our time. As the Book of Wisdom declares, "Our dying cannot be deferred, because it is fixed with a seal" (Ws 2:5/NAB). There may be certain mitigating factors that give the impression that a person may have escaped death's shadow, but that's all that it is: an impressive illusion! The Bible reminds us that it is appointed unto man once to die (Heb. 9:27), and its timing is set and on time!

Remember that on one's tombstone are the date of birth and the date of death. There is more than simply a grammatical reason as to why the two dates are separated by a dash. It is to remind us that the period of time from birth to death is a short span of time that moves with lightning speed and is over before we even know it! Zoom, zoom, zoom!

Do not let the Zoom Effect catch you off guard! Neither allow it to disturb your groove or dampen your zeal for life! Remember the words of

Yeshua, Jesus, who said that he came into the world that you and I might have life and have it more abundantly (John 10:10).

The question is, "What kind of life awaits us after the Zoom? Is the Beyond a more abundant life?" The only answer for the believer is, "Eternal life in the Afterlife is the best life!"

CHAPTER 4

The Existence and Nature of God

Belief is rooted in the concept of accepting and embracing something that is beyond our grasp, control, or ability to dictate terms. We equate faith with believing in something. In the classic movie *Miracle on 34th Street*, which seeks to establish the authenticity of Santa Claus, the protagonist, Kris Kringle, defines faith as "believing in something when common sense tells us not to." Faith or belief cannot be proven. It defies the senses. Common sense cannot figure it out! There is no scientific or empirical evidence that can be utilized in unraveling or solving the mysteries contained in a belief system. You either believe and accept it or deny and reject it. There is no middle ground.

Most believers embrace the notion of a Supreme Being who is the Creator/Progenitor of all things and "the ground of their being," in the words of philosopher Paul Tillich. Even though no one has ever seen or knows the full identity of this Divine Entity or its beginnings and end, the person who has come to a point of belief in such an Existence also accepts certain tenets of faith associated with that property. Yet, in the final analysis, all that is left for the believer to cling to is the confidence and blessed assurance that the One called God will prove to be all that the Godhead has been purported to be and all that one could ever hope for or desire.

From our earliest recollections, we were taught by our elders and parents and then reinforced through Sunday School and catechism lessons about the divine traits, characteristics, and attributes of a Supreme Being called *God*. We learned that God is essentially a Spirit (John 4:24) who has no beginning and no end. As a Spirit, God Is wind, breath, energy, and the life force. That Spirit cannot die or be destroyed, only transformed. If there was anything that each of us remembered about God from those early formative years, it was that God sat so high above us in Heaven that no one could equal Him or become anything close to incorporating His Essence and identity. God reigned over us, far beyond our comprehension or understanding.

Organized religion was so obsessed and preoccupied with intoxicating its believers through an indoctrination of God standing all alone, that it never concurrently taught us with the same vim and vigor about the relationship between God's identity, nature, and attributes on the one hand and us on the other — and that ultimately our calling on this earthly sojourn was to become the true sons and daughters of God, our Heavenly Parent, by fully embracing and becoming the Essence of God. Scripture says,

> See what love the Father [God] has bestowed on us that we may be called the children of God. Yet so we are. The reason the world does not know us is that it did not know him. Beloved, we are God's children now; what we shall be has not yet been revealed. We do know that when it is revealed we shall be like him, for we shall see him as he is (1 John 3:1–2/NAB).

The Word of God, then, is clear in boldly declaring the divine relationship between God and us. Thus, it follows that what God is we, too, are called to become and manifest. The Essence of God's nature in us is that which makes us "live, and move, and have our being" (Acts 17:28/KJV). Man and woman are essentially spirit beings robed in flesh, called to be human, rather than human beings seeking to become spiritual. Ancient wisdom had it correct from the start: "As above, so below. As within, so without."

It is by way of this profound understanding of the existence and nature of God that we come to an acute realization and actualization of what life is, how it is called to manifest itself in daily living, and what its ultimate end is after the spirit no longer resides in the corporeal or mortal frame that houses the Spirit of God.

There is hardly a believer alive who is not familiar with the content of Genesis 1:26, where God says, "Let us make man in our image, after our likeness." The first question to ponder is: Who is God (existence) and what is God (nature)?

As believers, we affirm that God is eternal, is One who has no beginning and no end. God is the penultimate expression of Spirit, a divine quality or attribute that is quintessential energy, boundless and ubiquitous. In God resides the fullness of all life. Everything that exists ebbs and flows from this Source. Anyone who is a recipient of this indwelling life-giving Spirit possesses a cell or seed of the divine presence. It is not watered down or diminished (although it is not fully developed) but has the same nature as the One from whence life comes. We define such a nature as spiritual birth. This runs concomitantly with physical birth in the womb.

If we believe that we are children of God (1 John 3), then we possess the same spiritual DNA as God, our Heavenly Parent. God is not simply God, the Creator of all things. God is our Parent! Unless you view God in this manner, you will not be able to comprehend your own identity and eternality.

The reason we, as human beings, have so much difficulty understanding the times and seasons of our lives is because we possess a mindset that is regulated and orchestrated by the temporal rather than the eternal. We cannot see life beyond our rationality.

Although the spiritual genetic traits, character, and nature of God are housed in a body (1 Cor. 3:16), it cannot be compromised or limited to the physical constraints of this realm. The Bible is replete with passages that distinguish the spiritual from the physical. We live, move, and have our being because God IS! Apart from the existence or nature of God, we are nothing. With God dwelling within us, we have the potential for becoming everything that God IS!

God, as Spirit, cannot be seen or ultimately known. God's presence can only be felt. Just because we cannot see God does not mean that God does not exist. A quick demonstration of this principle (introduced in the preceding chapter), called *Breath in the Hand,* is to hold your hand in front of your face and then blow your breath into it. You feel the breath but do not see it! No one can convince you that the breath is not real or existent; it simply cannot be seen. So it is with the existence or nature of God. You cannot see God, but God's presence is in every place where there is air, wind, or breath!

It is the same wind, air, or breath of which Genesis 2:7 speaks: "Then the Lord God formed a man from the dust of the ground and breathed into his nostrils the breath of life, and the man became a living being."

God, as Spirit, devoid of form, matter, and shape, created man and woman from the dust/dirt/clay of the Earth (thus giving them "substance"). God then "blew" breath within the corporeal mass in our mother's womb, and we became living souls/beings.

The spirit in man and woman is the very existence and nature of God. For it to be separate or distinct from the very nature of God would mean that God erred in defining the Divine Activity that brought man and woman into being. But God cannot lie and still be God!

The mystery of life is "if we live, we live for the Lord; and if we die, we die for the Lord. So, whether we live or die, we belong to the Lord" (Rom. 14:8/NIV). No need of us trying to figure out all of the intricate details of life or every aspect of life after death. One thing is for sure: Human life ceases at the time of physical death. But that which sustained human life — namely, the Spirit of God in us — continues to live as God lives, here, there, and everywhere.

Your presence on Earth in the flesh is a declaration of the Essence and Existence of the invisible God residing within you.

CHAPTER 5

Do You Believe?

God is Spirit, and those who worship him
must worship in Spirit and truth. — John 4:24/NAB

Beloved, do not trust every spirit but test the spirits to see
whether they belong to God, because many false prophets
have gone out into the world. — 1 John 4:1/NAB

It is truly amazing how we, as so-called educated people, have come to believe absolutely in the existence of something that has never been seen! Not only that, we have entered into an abiding relationship by communicating with that which has never dwelt among us in physical form. Most of us were taught in Sunday school, vacation Bible school, or catechetical classes (Confraternity of Christian Doctrine for Roman Catholics) that the essential and only nature of God is Spirit. Thus, we must relate to God "in Spirit and truth" (John 4:24). As such, God can neither be seen nor reduced to human understanding but merely approached by an ascent of faith. As the Word of God says,

Oh, the depth of the riches and wisdom and knowledge of God! How inscrutable are his judgments and how unsearchable his ways! "For who has known the mind of the Lord or who has been his counselor?" (Rom. 11:33–34/NAB).

The Bible says that no man or woman can see God and still live:

Then Moses said, "Do let me see your glory!" He answered, "I will make all my beauty pass before you, and in your presence. I will pronounce my name, Lord; I who show favors to whom I will, I who grant mercy to whom I will. But my face you cannot see, for no man sees me and still lives.

"Here," continued the Lord, "is a place near me where you shall station yourself on the rock. When my glory passes, I will set you in the hollow of the rock and I will cover you with my hand, so that you may see my back; but my face is not to be seen" (Exod. 33:18–23/NAB).

The Bible says, "Now faith is the substance of things hoped for, the evidence of things not seen" (Heb. 11:1). If that definition doesn't work, try applying Kris Kringle's definition of faith (as mentioned in a previous chapter) in his attempt to convince others that Santa Claus is real: "Faith is believing in something when common sense tells you not to" (*Miracle on 34th Street*). Do you believe in an Entity that cannot be seen with human eyes or touched with human hands?

While one's level of education plays no determining factor in ratifying or verifying the existence of God, education by way of indoctrination does play a role in convincing the believer that God exists — even without ever seeing or touching God! It begins from infancy, stretches through the years of adolescence, and is concretized and cemented in the adult mind. In the final analysis, those who embrace an awareness of God as Spirit and as the Life Breath by which they "live and move and have [their] being" (Acts 17:28) have come to believe that God exists in the universe and in man and woman:

"Do you not know that you are the temple of God, and that the Spirit of God dwells in you?" (1 Cor. 3:16). Again, reiterated in 1 Corinthians 6:19: "Do you not know that your body is a temple of the holy Spirit within you, whom you have from God, and that you are not your own?"

God, as Spirit, is absolute, unique, unchanging, and eternal. As believers, we speak also of God as omnipotent, omniscient, and omnipresent or ubiquitous. If these are the divine traits, attributes, and characteristics of God, then those created in the Divine Image and Likeness of God possess the same seeds.

How is it that we, as believers, who have embraced an understanding of God practically all our lives, fail to see the comparison between God's Life and the life of God in us? Do we believe that the spirit of God dwelling in man and woman is of the same essence as God? Are we confident that the spirit that dwelt within us still lives and exists when it leaves the body and spiritually ascends to return to the One who sent it forth? Yet, when a loved one physically dies, we believe that his or her life has ended or has taken on a form that is separate and distinct from us rather than still dwelling among us as God dwells in our midst. Once death occurs, the spirit of God in man and woman not only returns to God but becomes as God Is:

Beloved, we are God's children now; what we shall be has not yet been revealed. We do know that when it is revealed we shall be like him, for we shall see him as he is (1 John 3:2/NAB).

The point being emphasized is that God exists without us seeing or touching the God Self. Our faith has led us to that belief. There is no need for us to analyze it, because our level of indoctrination, honed and solidified over time, has led us to embrace God's presence within us. Yet, when it comes to the death of a loved one, we feel that there is such a separation and absence from us that we have to say "goodbye, farewell, or until we meet again."

But stop, think, and meditate for a moment. When did you or I ever say to God, living as pure Spirit, "goodbye, farewell, or until we meet again"? For the majority of us, that has never been the case. Man and woman, as the visible and tangible manifestation of the invisible and untouchable God were "postmarked" or stamped from the beginning as belonging to God (Rom. 14:7–8). Each one of us bears that spiritual "postmark." Thus, being God's property, the ultimate destiny of those born of the flesh is to one day be returned to the rightful Sender who initially "delivered" human beings to their temporary dwelling place: Earth. "And the dust returns to the earth as it once was, and the life breath returns to God who gave it" (Eccles. 12:7/NAB).

Only spirit can achieve that end. The question is, "Do you believe?"

CHAPTER 6

A Case of Apples to Oranges

None of us, as earthly creatures, can fathom the mind of God. The harder we try, the less we achieve in getting inside the "head" of God. Our finite or corporeal existence limits our capacity to penetrate the ubiquitous nature of God's existence and functionality. Any attempt, no matter how small or great, on our part to search out the labyrinthine ways of our Creator by juxtaposing them with our standards of knowledge and understanding is an exercise in futility. The apostle Paul reminds us in his Letter to the Romans: "Oh, how great are God's riches and wisdom and knowledge! How impossible it is for us to understand his decisions and his ways!" (Rom. 11:33/NLT).

The words of the prophet Isaiah further elucidate the point:

"For my thoughts are not your thoughts,
neither are your ways my ways,"
declares the Lord.
"As the heavens are higher than the earth,
so are my ways higher than your ways
and my thoughts than your thoughts" (Isa. 55:8–9/NIV).

When it comes to understanding the nature of life as it exists in God versus an understanding of earthly life as we have come to know and experience it, it is a case of comparing apples to oranges. The breath of life that God blew into the nostrils of mortal flesh at the moment of conception (Gen. 2:17) in our mother's womb is the presence of the Divine within each of us (1 Cor. 3:16). The Invisible becomes visible in man and woman, the Immortal dwells within mortality, the Incorruptible is housed in corruptibility.

At the point of physical death, the body, or tent, is "folded" to give way to that which is completely and totally invisible, imperishable, immortal, and incorruptible:

> For we know that if the earthly tent we live in is destroyed, we have a building from God, an eternal house in heaven, not built by human hands. Meanwhile we groan, longing to be clothed instead with our heavenly dwelling because when we are clothed, we will not be found naked. For while we are in this tent, we groan and are burdened, because we do not wish to be unclothed but to be clothed instead with our heavenly dwelling, so that what is mortal may be swallowed up by life. Now the one who has fashioned us for this very purpose is God, who has given us the Spirit as a deposit, guaranteeing what is to come.
>
> Therefore, we are always confident and know that as long as we are at home in the body we are away from the Lord. For we live by faith, not by sight. We are confident, I say, and would prefer to be away from the body and at home with the Lord
> (2 Cor. 5:1–8/NLT).

No one but God knows with exactitude the nature and context of life after the spirit exits the body. What form it takes on, where it goes or dwells, and how it continues to operate or function after physical death in a manner that is in complete alignment with the nature and presence of the Creator — these are the greatest mysteries of all.

What perplexes most people about death is F.E.A.R. of the unknown — what some have called *False Evidence Appearing Real*. The evidence contained in the Word of God says that we have nothing to fear other than a false notion of death itself. Even the psalmist describes death as a shadow: "Yea, though I walk through the valley of the shadow of death, I shall fear no evil" (Ps. 23:4/KJV). Yet, a mound of sermonic discourse and catechesis by the institutional Christian church, parroted and puppeteered by preachers and teachers of religion for centuries, has contributed immensely to brainwashing and instilling F.E.A.R. in the minds of believers that life after death is all about whether one goes to Heaven or hell. Layered on top of that "BS" (belief system!) is the myth that when the soul leaves the body, it will travel to some distant, faraway place beyond our sphere where it will either enjoy eternal life, if found worthy, or be condemned to a life of eternal torment in the fires of hell.

However, erroneous and misleading teachings about life after death that many believers have been taught and that have caught them "hook, line, and sinker" do not square up with the Word of God. In the words of Malcolm X, a lot of so-called believers have been "had, fooled, hoodwinked, and bamboozled"! If one carefully engages in a study of the Scriptures or Sacred Writings of many religious traditions regarding life after death and starts "connecting the dots," it soon becomes apparent that what is stated in the Word has not been consistently conveyed in message and action by mouth to bring comfort and reassurance to the believer. Rather, institutional preaching and teaching have served to further enslave and control the masses!

The Bible says that the earthly cannot enter into the eternal:

I declare to you, brothers and sisters, that flesh and blood cannot inherit the kingdom of God, nor does the perishable inherit the imperishable (1 Cor. 15:50/NIV).

... and the dust returns to the ground it came from, and the spirit returns to God who gave it (Eccles. 12:7/NIV).

We are confident, yes, well pleased rather to be absent from the body and to be present with the Lord (2 Cor. 5:8/NKJV).

Now when asked by the Pharisees when the kingdom of God would come, He [Jesus] answered them and said, "The kingdom of God does not come with observation; nor will they say, 'See here!' or 'See there!' For indeed, the kingdom of God is within you" (Luke 17:20–21/NKJV).

If we hold steadfast to the belief that the Kingdom of God, also known as the *Kingdom of Heaven,* resides within us, then we can have some sense of what it must be like to return unto the Source from whence we came and dwell within its fullness forever. We become one with the Source and accompany it wherever it goes and in whatever it accomplishes.

Accordingly, there would be no need for the spirit or soul to "go" anywhere, due to the ubiquitous nature of spirit. When the spirit leaves the body and spiritually ascends, it returns to God and is embedded in God's Essence for eternity.

The only mystery awaiting us is uncovering at what level of individual consciousness we will come to know and realize that, in physical death, we become ONE AND THE SAME as God.

In the meantime, any attempt to search the unsearchable or to "unscrew" the inscrutable is like comparing apples to oranges!

CHAPTER 7

We Are More Than What We Think

Created in the image and likeness of God, we are essentially spirit beings robed in flesh. That which makes us "live, move, and have our being" (Acts 17:28) did not originate in the flesh. It came forth from the Essence of God, which is Pure Spirit, and fully known by God. That means that you and I have existed in spirit since time immemorial IN God. Each of us existed simply as an idea in God's mind until the point when He decided to create a soul and incarnate it as a fertilized seed in a woman's womb. In the case of the biblical character Jeremiah (Jer. 1), for eternity God had him and all his prophetic power as an idea in His mind, yet when the opportune time came, Jeremiah's soul was substantiated and he was born into the world.

God has known us from all eternity because we were created out of God's Spirit. When the Old Testament biblical figure Jeremiah, at the threshold of his youth, engaged in a conversation with God about feeling ill-prepared to undertake a call to prophetic ministry that would require more than he could handle, the Lord God said unto him, "Before I formed you in the womb, I knew you. Before you were born, I dedicated you, a prophet to the nations I appointed you" (Jer. 1:5/NAB).

The assertion by God clearly indicates that Jeremiah had a prior existence in the Essence of God before he was conceived in his mother's womb. It was not as an individualized entity but part of the content of God's nature. Second, God knows us before physical conception, because God knows Self.

At the moment of human conception, God breathed the breath of life into corporeal mass at the initiation of its formation in our mother's womb, and we became living beings (Gen. 2:7). It was at that point that you and I took on a unique, individualized persona that would distinguish each one of us from the rest of us. We are more than what we think!

Where there is spirit, there is life. When the spirit is absent from the body, there is no life! This profound understanding is classically illustrated in the Old Testament, where the prophet Ezekiel has a vision of the Dry Bones:

> The hand of the Lord came upon me, and he led me out in the spirit of the Lord and set me in the center of the plain, which was now filled with bones. He made me walk among them in every direction so that I saw how many they were on the surface of the plain. How dry they were! He asked me: "Son of man, can these bones come to life?" "Lord God," I answered, "you alone know that." Then he said to me: "Prophesy over these bones, and say to them: Dry bones, hear the word of the Lord! Thus says the Lord God to these bones: See! I will bring spirit into you, that you may come to life. I will put sinews upon you, make flesh grow over you, cover you with skin, and put spirit in you so that you may come to life and know that I am the Lord." I prophesied as I had been told, and even as I was prophesying, I heard a noise; it was a rattling as the bones came together, bone joining bone. I saw the sinews and the flesh come upon them, and the skin cover them, but there

was no spirit in them. Then he said to me: "Prophesy to the spirit, prophesy, son of man, and say to the spirit: From the four winds come, O spirit, and breathe into these slain that they may come to life." I prophesied as he told me, and the spirit came into them; they came alive and stood upright, a vast army (Ezek. 37:1–10).

This provocative scriptural passage needs a little more weight applied. It is chock full of sermonic content! I will try my best to refrain from preaching while unpacking it, although I know it will be extremely difficult to do so. Please bear with me!

The prophet Ezekiel, caught up in the snare of an apocalyptic moment, was led "out in the spirit of the Lord and set … in the center of the plain," where he experienced the manifestation of the divine presence, known as a *theophany*. He was enraptured and transfixed by his conversation with God. In the midst of examining a plain filled with the mortal remains of soldiers who had perished in battle, he was stunned by just how dry the bones appeared. "How dry they were," exclaimed the prophet. They conveyed every indication that the men had been dead for quite some time after battle. Their form was devoid of sinew, skin, and flesh and had disintegrated to such an extent that their substance had been reduced to bones.

The Lord God asked Ezekiel, "son of man, can these dry bones come to life?" The prophet, unfamiliar with the process of how life is restored, simply responded by putting his complete trust and confidence in God. "Surely," he must have thought to himself, "if anyone can do it, God can!" Ezekiel knew it was beyond his knowledge or understanding in that moment to unravel the mystery of life and death.

When it comes to the things of God, namely, how God thinks, acts, and reacts in the course of human events, we need to simply realize that trying to figure it all out is above our pay grade! The Word of God confirms it: "Oh, the depth of the riches and wisdom and knowledge of God! How inscrutable are his judgments and how unsearchable his ways! 'For who has known the mind of the Lord or who has been his counselor?'" (Rom. 11:33–34/NAB).

The Lord God tells the prophet to "prophesy over the bones, and say to them: Dry bones, hear the word of the Lord! Thus says the Lord God to these bones: See! I will bring spirit into you that you may come to life." Has it every crossed your mind that dry bones cannot hear a thing? How could they possibly hear what the prophet was speaking to them? It must have happened intuitively. Here, we arrive at the first level of understanding about mortal flesh. Human flesh, in and of itself, cannot exist without form or structure.

God tells the prophet to speak first and foremost to that which holds the flesh in place, namely, the bones. While bones in and of themselves do not possess life, they are an essential part of the human structure in order for the body to receive life. The Word of God was not solely addressing the inanimate but the animate that would follow it. The process of initiation to restore life began with bone connecting to bone.

Before the dry bones could serve as the skeletal structure for the re-robing of mortal flesh, there had to be an adherence to the Word of God. As the Book of Proverbs states, "Trust in the Lord with all thine heart; and lean not unto thine own understanding. In all thy ways acknowledge him, and he shall direct thy paths" (Prov. 3:5–6/KJV). This is the next level of understanding: having faith and trusting in God's Word. If God said it, that settles it!

How true Ezekiel found it to be! After prophesying as the Lord God commanded, he "heard a noise; it was a rattling as the bones came together, bone joining bone." He later witnessed (in the vision) sinews and flesh coming upon the bones and skin covering them. But there was one major problem: "there was no spirit in them."

Note that the phrase, "I will put sinews upon you, make flesh grow over you, [and] cover you with skin" (verse 6a), is sandwiched between two definitive declarations by the Lord God: "See! I will bring spirit into you" (verse 5) and "put spirit in you so that you may come to life and know that I am the Lord" (verse 6b). Why does an emphasis on "spirit" precede and follow the restoration of the physical form? It is to remind us that a person can even have "a body built by Fisher" (a famous automaker metaphor), but, with no spirit present within, it is good as dead. This is the third level of understanding: Mortal flesh needs the presence of the invisible spirit of God in order to live.

Then the Lord God said to the prophet, "Prophesy to the spirit, prophesy, son of man, and say to the spirit: From the four winds come, O spirit, and breathe into these slain that they may come to life." This is the fourth level of understanding about life after death. It was only when the breath returned and entered into the bodies of the slain soldiers that "they came alive and stood upright, a vast army."

The profound moral of the story, shrouded in a powerful vision experience, is that all life comes from God and only God can bestow and restore it. God is the Source of life itself. The essence of life is the Spirit of the invisible God residing in mortal flesh. All of life originates and ends in God. No power or principality has control or ownership over it. It belongs to God and to those to whom God imparts a portion of His Spirit. Since physical death is not the author of life and has no ownership or control over life, it can lay no claim over it. Ultimately, death will be swallowed up in victory. As the Bible declares, "Where, O death, is your victory? Where, O death, is your sting?" (1 Cor. 15:55/NAB).

It would make no sense for the invisible God to create us in the divine image and likeness so as to manifest His presence on Earth, only to have us surrender that life in physical death without picking it up again in the After-life. It would be a denial of the very nature of God, which is eternal. We are either of God or not of God! If you and I believe we are of God, we live on after physical death in a new state of existence after we "cross over." If we do not believe, it means that when the Zoom Effect comes crashing down upon our mortal frame, there will be no anticipation of a bright future with God in the company of our loved ones forever!

Let us remember who we are and what we are. We are more than what we think!

CHAPTER 8

A Time and a Season

There is a time for everything, and a season for every activity
under the heavens: a time to be born and a time to die.
— Eccles. 3:1–2/NIV

It is amazing that science, in all of its brilliance, has discovered birth control but not death control! How is it that man and woman possess the intelligence or ability to disrupt life but haven't figured out how to sustain it eternally? It is because death is unavoidable! There is an appointed time and season for death to cast its shadow upon our lives, yet some of us live as if it is unlikely to occur or that it does not have our name written on it. But there will come that moment for all of us when "the silver cord is snapped and the golden bowl is broken, the pitcher is shattered at the spring, and the broken pulley falls into the well and the dust [from whence our corporeal frame was formed and fashioned] returns to the earth as once it was" (Eccles. 12:6–7a/NAB).

It is inevitable that all of us, born of the flesh, will eventually succumb to the forces of physical death. One phase does not come into this world without being accompanied by death. It is not a question of either/or but of both/and! We all will have our personal rendezvous with death! No exceptions! No exemptions! No one knows exactly when that moment will come and how it will occur. Only one thing is for certain: It is known to God and God alone! God, in His divine omniscience, has a multitude of ideas of the when and where of each person's death, but which of those ideas becomes real is determined by human-caused circumstances.

None of us should live our lives in a state of fear, anxiety, worry, or pre-occupation, wondering if today will be the last day of our physical days on Earth. We should live each day of our lives as if it were the first, the last, and the only day.:

Qoheleth, the king over Israel in Jerusalem, applied his mind "to search and investigate in wisdom all things that are done under the sun" (Eccles. 1:13/NAB). Among his conclusions: "I recognized that there is nothing better than to be glad and to do well during life. For every man, moreover, to eat and drink and enjoy the fruit of all his labor is a gift of God. I recognized that whatever God does will endure forever; there is no adding to it or taking from it. Thus has God done that he may be revered. What now is has already been; what is to be, already is; and God restores what would otherwise be displaced" (Eccles. 3:12–15/NAB).

"It is appointed for men once to die, and after this the judgment" (Heb. 9:27/NAB). And that's speaking of man in the generic sense! No one can escape it!

Nothing is to be gained by trying to falsify death or dismissing its reality. It will come for each of us as day follows night and night follows day! The question is: Will we be ready when that day suddenly comes upon us "like labor pains upon a pregnant woman, and [there] will [be] no escape" (1 Thess. 5:3/NAB)?

Denial of its existence has no place in the life of the believer when it comes to the inevitability of death. To think otherwise would be preposterous and an exercise in futility! It will surely come! And when it comes, it will be our time and no one else's!

When one gets right down to it, there is no such thing as "dying before one's time"! When a person dies, that is his or her time. Otherwise, who's time would it be? Anyone but yours or mine? That, too, is vanity: "God has made everything appropriate to its time, and has put the timeless into their hearts, without men's ever discovering, from beginning to end, the work which God has done" (Eccles. 3:11/NAB).

Another common mistake often made by the believer when speaking about a person's death is that God's heart was so moved that God "called" him or her from Earth to eternity in the ordinary course of daily living or in the midst of suffering or tragedy. The ill-informed mind would sympathize in attributing such a position to God. Surely, God must know just how much the human heart can bear. The believer rationalizes it by thinking it would be far better for God to snatch that person from Earth to Heaven rather than allowing him or her to endure continued suffering and excruciating pain. In short, the mistaken belief is that God's heart was so moved by a person's intense suffering that He gently closed his or her eyes and took the person away from us. That, too, is vanity!

The apocryphal Book of Wisdom, often referred to as a *deuterocanonical* text in biblical circles, states it clearly: "God did not make death, nor does he rejoice in the destruction of the living. For he fashioned all things that they might have being; and the creatures of the world are wholesome and there is not a destructive drug among them" (Ws 1:13–14/NAB).

God does not call any of us unto the fullness of the Godhead, no matter how much a person may be suffering or whether that person be good or evil, for God "makes his sun rise on the bad and the good, and causes rain to fall on the just and the unjust" (Matt. 5:45/NAB), until after physical death has occurred. It is at that moment that we return unto the Source from whence we came (Eccles. 12:7b) and live with God and in God for eternity. According to the Word of God, not only do we return to God but ultimately become subsumed or embedded in the totality of God's Divine Essence and become like or as God Is (1 John 3:2).

Another illogical concept associated with God that makes no sense whatsoever is when someone says, while eulogizing a decedent, "We loved [the person], but God loved him/her best!" Upon serious reflection, how can such a statement bring comfort to the bereaved? Is God's love so callous and insensitive that it would snuff out the life of a loved one created in God's image and likeness? Is that how God expresses the depths of the divine love for us so as to distinguish and separate it from the love that we possess? The thinking behind such reasoning is that, if the bereaved can attribute a loved one's passing to God, who knows what is best, then it makes the death easier to digest by putting it in God's hands. That, too, is vanity!

A final thought: There is no need to even begin to imagine what life on Earth would be like without our physical presence. That, too, is vanity! Life will go on with or without us. Another generation will take over and continue where we left off! While others may have preceded us in death, there will come a time when we will precede others. Having had the benefit of witnessing the physical death of others and its impact, we should use those occasions as a reflection on what our lives will mean to others after we have exited Stage Left and taken our place in the annals of history.

There is a time and a season for all of us! And that is *not* vanity!

CHAPTER 9

A Heavenly Paradigm Shift

There are very few things in life that are non-negotiables. For many, the notion of Heaven ranks at the top of the list. If there is anything that believers do not want someone to mess or tamper with, it is their cherished beliefs that are the bedrock of their faith. The majority of people of faith believe that, while Heaven is not a physical place, it is a spiritual destination with an eternal dwelling place where souls go after their departure from Earth.

Most believers would think it preposterous, if not blasphemous, to suggest that Heaven could actually exist right here on Earth! Such retorts as "That's absolutely impossible; you are bordering on heresy!" or "After all, how can Heaven be seen or understood as anything other than extraterrestrial?" would gush forth from their mouths!

The challenge faced by this author in *Beyond the Zoom: The Afterlife* is presenting a viable alternative to the "pie in the sky" notion (theory) of the Afterlife by presenting Heaven in the context of *returning unto the Source from whence we came* (Eccles. 12:7b). It means ultimately being present wherever God is at all times and in all ways. The pathway to understanding and unraveling the profound mystery of life after death can be accomplished by unpacking biblical citations that clearly demonstrate in a convincing way that Heaven and God are one and the same!

All life originates in God, the Creator of all things. It is from this One Source that man and woman emanate and find their beginning and end. While that which makes humans "live, move, and have their being" (Acts 17:28), is essentially spiritual in nature, that which houses (earthen vessel) the spirit does not come forth out of God but out of man and woman (corporeal matter), who serve as cocreators with God. The Book of Ecclesiastes 12:7 sheds light on this mystery: "The dust shall return to the earth as it once was, but the spirit or life breath shall return unto God [the Creator] who gave it."

We read in 2 Corinthians 5:8, "To be absent from the body is to be present with the Lord." What is it to be "absent"? It is the spirit not dwelling in the body. When the spirit in man and woman, that is, the Essence of God, is no longer present in the body, where does it go? It goes to be "present" wherever God dwells. The Word of God is definitive: Once a person "expires" at the point of the breath exiting the body, it returns to the Source from whence it came. The word *expire* has its origins in the Latin language. It is a combination of the prefix *ex*, to go out, and the verb *spirare*, to breathe. If that be the case, then nothing can exit the body unless it is breathing and therefore living!

The question for the ages is: When the spirit exits the body, where is its final resting place? If God is omnipresent or ubiquitous and thus is anywhere and everywhere at the same time, why would the spirit (soul) need to take an extended, out-of-this-world journey to return to its Source? If God is eternal and is present right here on Earth, why would the spirit of a deceased person be required to leave this terrestrial plane to enjoy eternal life in another realm? Could not Heaven be where God is?

Jesus was asked by the Pharisees when the Kingdom of God would come. Most, if not all, biblical scholars would agree that the Kingdom of Heaven and the Kingdom of God are one and the same, or synonymous. Jesus said in reply, "The coming of the kingdom of God cannot be observed, and no one will announce, 'Look, here it is,' or, 'There it is.' For behold, the kingdom of God is among you" (Luke 17:20–21). Other translations render the phrase as the Kingdom of God is "within you" or "in your midst." It all depends on which Gospel translation or version you read.

If the Word of God is authentic in saying that we are temples of God and the Holy Spirit dwells within us (1 Cor. 3:16), then we need not look any further for the presence of the Kingdom of God than within us. The reason we cannot fully experience the Kingdom of Heaven on Earth is due to a flawed human nature that fails to see the God within each and every person (including ourselves) created in God's image and likeness. The "powers of this dark world and the spiritual forces of evil in the heavenly realms" (Eph. 6:12/NIV) are constantly at war with the presence of the spirit of God residing in us. While God is drawing us ever closer to Himself, the Prince of Darkness and his minions are tugging us in the opposite direction. The noted Jesuit priest Teilhard de Chardin, a prolific writer, scientist, theologian, philosopher, teacher, and paleontologist, said it best: "Release the imprisoned splendor within you."

While we can have a foretaste or experience of Heaven in the flesh, we cannot embrace it in its fullness until the body succumbs to the forces of death and the spirit is reunited with its Source and Origin, as it was in the beginning. Such a process of spiritual transition and transformation cannot be fathomed by the human mind. It is far too great a mystery to be fully understood in human terminology. But one thing is for sure, according to the Word of God: "What we shall be has not yet been revealed. We do know that when it is revealed we shall be like [or as] Him, for we shall see

Him as He is" (1 John 3:2/NAB).

The dilemma faced in acquiring a whole new spiritual way of thinking (Rom. 12:2) and putting on the new self (Eph. 4:23–24/NAB) to embrace a new paradigm of Heaven is discovering how to throw out the bathwater without throwing out the baby! In other words, how does one jettison the traditional myths surrounding the Afterlife yet cling to one's belief in an afterlife that is biblically sound and reassuring in its promises? The truth lies "in the pudding" by "connecting the dots" that remind us that, in death, life is changed, not ended. There is an afterlife after the Zoom!

CHAPTER 10

The Water, Pitcher, and Glasses Demonstration

For as a man thinketh in his heart, so is he!
— Prov. 23:7/KJV

What the mind can conceive and believe, it can achieve.
— Norman Vincent Peale

Let this mind be in you, which was also in Christ Jesus.
— Phil. 2:5/KJV

Heaven is closer than you think! It is within your grasp if your mind can conceive it and believe it! Such an assertion flies in the face of what believers have come to know about that place one enters at the conclusion of one's earthly life. After physical death, most of us anticipate "going somewhere" above and beyond this terrestrial plane, where an abyss, void, or chasm exists that separates the living from the dead. Some even imagine that it will be a material place with twelve gates to the city, walls of jasper, and streets of purest gold (Rev. 21:18) where we will walk around in long, white robes, clad in golden slippers and living in a palatial mansion on the corner of Grace Boulevard and Mercy Street! How can such indelible images of Heaven ever be erased from the fundamentalist believer's mind so as to envision a state of "heavenly habitation not made by hands" (2 Cor. 5:1–2). Pushing the envelope, has anyone ever wondered by what means or in what manner we are to be transported to that place in the sky in the "sweet by and by" once we die?

It seems a majority of so-called believers don't even question such assertions or have any doubt about their validity in Scripture. After all, how many preachers and catechists have they encountered on their faith walk that hammered such images into their heads as pure doctrine? It is no wonder that so many people are afraid to die, wondering if they have lived lives worthy enough of entering "the pearly gates"! In many instances, the believer has been intimidated by mind games perpetrated by those who call themselves gurus interceding between God and humankind.

The mind can play tricks on you if you allow it to be constantly manipulated and filled with concepts and images that do not align with biblical teaching or find reality in truth. Metaphysically, "the mind is the seat of perception of the things we see, hear, and feel. It is through the mind that we see the beauties of the earth and sky, of music, of art, in fact, of everything. That silent shuttle of thought working in and out through cell and nerve weaves into one harmonious whole the myriad moods of mind, and we call it life." These words are from Charles Filmore, the founder of Unity.

Without the mind of the believer realizing it, church doctrine is often formulated and constructed to keep the masses in line, strike fear in and intimidate church adherents, and flex ecclesiastical muscle to prevent people from going helter-skelter with homespun theology. For example, it is widely known that for centuries the Roman Catholic Church vigorously taught and held firmly to the doctrine of Limbo, supposedly an after-death dwelling place where unbaptized children ended up as a result of parental neglect by failing to have the Sacrament of Baptism administered to the children shortly after their birth. Limbo proved to be a doctrinal teaching with no biblical foundation but was employed as a scare tactic to stir the conscience of parents to be good Catholics. Needless to say, most Catholics drank the Kool-Aid!

When it comes to a belief in Heaven, we need to undergo a spiritual transformation and renewal of the mind (Rom. 12:2). Our minds need to align themselves with what the Scriptures say about the Kingdom of Heaven, not with a tenet of faith based on what some uninformed preacher or teacher has passed on to us without it undergoing exegetical or herme-neutical scrutiny.

Jesus declared that the Kingdom of God (synonymous with the King-dom of Heaven) cannot be observed, when asked by the Pharisees of its imminence. "Neither shall they say, lo here! Or, lo there! For, behold, the kingdom of God is within you" (Luke 17:20–21/KJV). What is the Kingdom of God (Kingdom of Heaven), and what does it mean for that kingdom to be within you or in your midst?

The Kingdom of God is where God dwells and the realm from which God operates and orders all things into being. That realm is Heaven, whether we have ever perceived or considered it as such. Wherever God is, so is Heaven! For God to live outside of Heaven and still be God would be like a fish living out of water and still surviving and remaining true to its nature. God's Essence is Pure Spirit, and that is everywhere. It is the same Spirit that was breathed into the nostrils of man and woman and made them living beings. Thus, God's Spirit in man and woman that makes them "live, move, and have their being" is essentially the Kingdom of Heaven dwelling within them.

If you believe that the Spirit of God (spiritual) is encased in the physical form of man and woman (made of material from the Earth), why would it not follow that Heaven is embedded in Earth and, thus, Heaven is within us? To put it plainly, Heaven is in our midst! It is not a place above and beyond our world but a place of spiritual habitation that can be realized and actualized in the here and now, within us, albeit in an imperfect way while still robed in the body. It should not be a place that is unfamiliar to us. It should be a place that we gradually come to embrace as we gain greater self-awareness of our divine origins and place in the world. It must be a goal that we strive to reach each day so as to inherit eternal life. As the great American theologian Dr. Norman Vincent Peale trumpeted, "What the mind can conceive and believe, it can achieve."

Let us explore this concept even further. God, as Spirit, breathes or pours life into a vessel of clay (man and woman) and makes them living beings. That which makes man and woman "live, move, and have their being" is the Essence of God's divine nature dwelling within them. Since God does not possess physical form or traits, those created as mortals become the substantial and visible form of God that can be seen, touched, embraced, and loved. When the mortal frame reaches the point of physical death, that which was breathed or poured into man and woman returns unto the Source/Creator from whence it came and becomes one with Him, embedded in the same Essence of the One who sent it forth in the flesh.

This profound spiritual principle is reflected in the Book of Ecclesiastes 12:7: "Then shall the dust return to the earth as it was: and the spirit shall return unto God who gave it" (KJV).

A wonderful demonstration to illustrate this principle is "The Clear

Pitcher of Water and Two Glasses Demonstration." The Clear Pitcher of Water represents and contains the Essence of God, the Creator and Heavenly Parent. The two Glasses (one textured/colored and the other clear glass) respectively represent the human form — first, coming forth born in sin and shaped in iniquity and, second, called to spiritually perfect itself by becoming one with God.

Once you have established the principle of God creating man and woman in His "image and likeness" (Gen. 1:26), which pertains solely to humankind's spiritual nature, take the Pitcher of Water (God's Essence) and pour some of the Water from the Clear Pitcher into the textured/colored glass (representing man's physical nature, formed from the dust of the Earth, and humanity's sinful condition and as a reference to Psalm 51:5/KJV: "Behold, I was shapen in iniquity; and in sin did my mother conceive me").

Then pose the question: "Is there a difference between the Nature of the Water in the Clear Pitcher and the nature of the water in the textured/colored glass?" The answer is obviously "No!"

Next, slowly pour the water from the textured/colored glass into the clear glass to symbolically demonstrate the spiritual progression in a person's life from a sinful to a perfected state as God originally intended it before sin invaded the planet. At the point of physical death, the Word of God says that man's mortal frame returns to the Earth as dust, but the spirit or the life breath returns unto God who gave it. As you pour the water from the clear glass back into the Clear Pitcher of Water, ask the question: "Can anyone distinguish or separate the water that has been poured back into the Clear Pitcher from the Water that was in the Clear Pitcher?" Again, the answer is obviously "No!"

And so it is when the Spirit of God (eternal) is poured or breathed into the flesh of man and woman (finite) at the moment of physical conception. They become God's substantial presence on Earth in bodily form, albeit in an imperfected state. Man and woman's ultimate goal is to transform their sinful nature (as symbolized by the textured/colored glass) by obedience to God's Word and, through a spiritual process, be poured, like a libation, into the clear glass by striving to bring themselves into divine alignment with God's plan and purpose for their life.

But when that physical life has completed its earthly course, it returns unto God and becomes ONE and the SAME as God. They become ONE IN SPIRIT. It is not that there are zillions of spirits in perpetual motion *surrounding* God's presence, but they all function in eternal activity in the Oneness of God.

The Kingdom of Heaven germinates in the mind and reaches fruition when the earth (body) releases the spirit (God in us) to return to the Source from whence it came to become ONE ENTITY for all eternity.

CHAPTER 11

Out of Sight, but Still in Mind

In physical death, there is no spiritual separation or departure between those who have died and those who are left behind on Earth. Out of sight does not mean out of mind! There is a change in relationship, not kinship! What often causes excruciating pain to bereaved families at the passing of a loved one is a belief or feeling that they have lost that deceased person forever to the ages. However, no physical contact any longer does not preclude spiritual communion.

God is Pure Spirit and is not limited by time and space. As those created in the divine image and likeness of God, we have uninterrupted and unbroken access to God at any time and in any place. God, as Spirit, is not separated or distant from us but is an ever-present eternal Entity. God, who cannot be seen, exists in the mind and heart of those who believe. How can we hold, on the one hand, to a belief that we can commune with God, even though we cannot see God, and yet, on the other hand, cling to the notion that just because someone has died we lose contact or interaction with them because they are no longer physically present among us?

In many cases, when it comes to our belief system, our orthodoxy does not equate with our orthopraxis. An easier way of saying it is, our faith does not match our practice. Created as children of God by our Heavenly Parent, we often act like distant relatives or strangers rather than inheritors of the promises of God. Our vertical relationship with God is only validated by a horizontal relationship with each other, both in life and death. Death does not end a relationship between those who have died and those who remain on Earth. It only strengthens and solidifies a union that can never be broken!

Unfortunately, most human beings have become so absorbed, obsessed, and preoccupied with earthly living and mundane pursuits that any thought of severing ties with this Earth via death is abhorrent, distasteful, and to be avoided at all costs! Yet, what one often fails to realize is that death is not about an end. It is a gateway to a new horizon for a deceased loved one that inaugurates a new, unparalleled love relationship with those left behind.

The challenge to the believer is to see all of life, both the temporal and the eternal, as a single, seamless multicolored garment of various hues and textures, not as broken fragments or disjointed pieces. With such an understanding, life never ends, even when others precede us in the "sleep" of death. Rather, life takes on a totally spiritual manifestation and operation in its ability to connect those who remain on the Earth in fleshly form and those who have transitioned — mirroring the way God, as Spirit, relates to us each and every moment of our human existence.

The apostle Paul admonishes us to "acquire a whole new spiritual way of thinking" (Rom. 12:2), especially if we are to grasp the things of the spirit that make absolutely no common sense to the human mind. The mind is constantly playing tricks on us by discouraging us from embracing anything that cannot be seen or touched. We fall prey to our worst fears and wreak mental havoc upon ourselves by not allowing our faith to stand in the central position of informing our outlook on life. We allow external forces to "steal, kill, and destroy" the promises God has made to us, His children, namely, that He would never abandon or forsake us but remain always with us. If that be the case, then those who have died and returned "to the Source from whence they came" (Eccles. 12:7) are always with us.

Sounds too good to be true? You bet your sweet bippy it does! But that is the beauty of mystery. Some things the human mind cannot fathom. What matters is that our mind, heart, and soul are anchored in the Lord!

If you believe that God is in every human being ever created — as a temple of God where the Holy Spirit dwells (1 Cor. 3:16) — then it should not be too much of a challenge to come to grips with an understanding that all can return to the same God and become ONE in God, the Progenitor of all things.

You don't have to see it to believe it. Out of sight does not mean out of mind!

CHAPTER 12

Heaven Is a Metaphor

Heaven has often been portrayed as an out-of-this-world place where the deceased go after living a virtuous and honorable life on Earth. Yet, what has been described throughout the ages as the material attributes of the place of eternal rest often do not align themselves with the Scriptures. Many Christian believers have come to embrace a notion of the Afterlife as consisting of "going up yonder" somewhere. Heaven as a physical place where souls ascend to inhabit a "mansion" in the sky simply does not exist. Such descriptions of Heaven are metaphoric rather than real. Most of what has been preached or taught for centuries about the existence of a place called Heaven have been drawn from images and symbolic expressions lifted from the Book of Revelation.

The Beloved Apostle, John, while exiled on an island called *Patmos*, had some extraordinary visions that were not grounded in reality, consisting of imaginary renderings of a heavenly realm. Unfortunately, those visions over time gradually became so etched in the psyche of believers as well as entrenched in the catechesis and teachings of so many churches that they were warranted as being authentic or actual.

The New American Bible editors' introduction to the Book of Revelation sets the framework for approaching the book's content and understanding its meaning:

> The Apocalypse, or Revelation of John, the last book of the Bible, is one of the most difficult to understand because it abounds in unfamiliar and extravagant symbolism, which at best appears unusual to the modern reader. Symbolic language, however, is one of the chief characteristics of apocalyptic literature, of which this book is an outstanding example.
>
> This book contains an account of visions in symbolic and allegorical language borrowed extensively from the Old Testament, especially Ezekiel, Zechariah, and Daniel. Whether or not these visions were real experiences of the author or simply literary conventions employed by him is an open question.
>
> This much, however, is certain: symbolic descriptions are not to be taken as literal descriptions, nor is symbolism meant to be pictured realistically.

With that appreciation, we can better understand what John witnessed during the stages of his vision: "I, John, your brother, who share with you the distress, the kingdom, and the endurance we have in Jesus, found myself on the island called Patmos because I proclaimed God's word and gave testimony to Jesus. I was caught up in spirit on the Lord's Day and heard behind me a voice as loud as a trumpet, which said, 'Write on a scroll what you see and send it to the seven churches [of Asia Minor]'" (Rev. 1:9–11/ NAB).

Obviously, the apostle John, under duress and feeling a personal sense of anxiety, frustration, and distress, needed to be reminded and reassured that he and other believers of "The Way" (prior to being called *Christians*) had made the right decision by following Jesus. The subsequent visions that followed occurred while he was "caught up in the spirit."

In that light, let us examine some of the images that have been fashioned and systematized by preachers, teachers, and catechists throughout the centuries in conjuring up a contrived notion of the properties of Heaven as an eternal dwelling place where we go to live with God after death. Those images, as stated earlier, are drawn particularly from apocalyptic passages in the Book of Revelation as well as from the Gospel of John, chapter 14, where it references *mansions*.

The Book of Revelation consists of twenty-two chapters. It is in the twenty-first chapter that the Scriptures record John's account of what has been described as a vision of the heavenly realm personified as a New Jerusalem:

> Then I saw a new heaven and a new earth. The former heaven and the former earth had passed away, and the sea was no more. I also saw the holy city, a new Jerusalem, coming down out of heaven from God, prepared as a bride adorned for her husband. I heard a loud voice from the throne saying, "Behold, God's dwelling is with the human race. He will dwell with them and they will be his people and God himself will always be with them [as their God]. He will wipe every tear from their eyes, and there shall be no more death or mourning, wailing or pain, [for] the old order has passed away."
>
> He took me in spirit to a great, high mountain and showed me the holy city Jerusalem coming down out of heaven from God. It gleamed with the splendor of God. Its radiance was like that of a precious stone, like jasper, clear as crystal. It had a massive, high wall, with twelve gates where twelve angels were stationed and on

which names were inscribed, [the names] of the twelve tribes of the Israelites. There were three gates facing east, three north, three south, and three west. The walls of the city had twelve courses of stones as its foundation, on which were inscribed the twelve names of the twelve apostles of the Lamb.

The wall was constructed of jasper, while the city was pure gold, clear as glass. The twelve gates were twelve pearls, each of the gates made from a single pearl; and the street of the city was pure gold, transparent as glass (Rev. 21:1–4, 10–14, 18, 21/NAB).

A close examination of the above text conveys a sense that John was caught up in the Parousia, or end times. In that moment, he envisioned a time when Heaven and Earth, as he had known them, no longer existed. He "saw a new heaven and a new earth … [and] the holy city, a new Jerusalem, coming down out of heaven from God."

The confusion in understanding starts at that point. Are Heaven and the New Jerusalem one and the same concept or entity, or are they different? The reading of the text gives the impression that the latter proceeded or came out of the former. Whatever the interpretation, one thing is for sure: All of the metaphoric language, symbols, and imagery attributed to Heaven are associated with the New Jerusalem.

The situation is further complicated by the vision placing emphasis on a city "coming down out of heaven," implying that man and woman are to inherit such a place where God dwells with the human race. The New Jerusalem is presented as a city abounding with opulent material extravagance, the foundations of its walls "decorated with every precious stone," with the first course of stone being of jasper. The streets were of pure gold, transparent as glass, replete with twelve entry gates of pearl.

Yet, "God's dwelling is with the human race," which implies that man and woman's dwelling is with and in God. The passage says "[God] will dwell with them and they will be his people and God himself will always be with them [as their God]."

The real question is: When the spirit or soul exits the body, does it leave its mortal frame only to dwell in another physical dwelling place?

Our faith teaches us that, in order for the soul to inherit the Kingdom of God (also known interchangeably as the *Kingdom of Heaven*), the flesh must be shed. Once the spirit of the Living God residing within mortal flesh leaves the body, it is able to return to the Source from whence it came (Eccles. 12:7). The apostle Paul reminds the believer, "This I declare, brothers: flesh and blood cannot inherit the kingdom of God, nor does corruption inherit incorruption" (1 Cor. 15:50/NAB). The obverse, therefore, would be true, namely, that the spirit cannot dwell in anything that is physical, at the same time, and inherit eternal life.

One of the greatest Church Doctors and thinkers in early Christianity, Saint John Chrysostom, provides comfort for those who feel the anguish and distress of saying "goodbye, farewell, or until we meet again" to those who have died: "Those whom we love and lose are no longer where they were before. They are now wherever we are."

A paradigm shift in the way we view "dwelling place" is required to possess a deeper understanding of Heaven. Heaven is not a "place" but a "state" of spiritual existence. The Book of Ecclesiastes 12:7 (NAB) reassures us: "And the dust returns to the earth as it once was, and the life breath returns to God who gave it." If you and I were made in the image and likeness of God and came forth from the Oneness of God, then why would it not make sense that, in the end, we will return unto the Source from whence we came? That is the "home" to which we should aspire: to live in the fullness of the Essence of God forever.

Thus, Heaven is God and God is Heaven! Don't anticipate any "mansions" in the sky in the "sweet by and by." Heaven is about relationship, not ownership! Returning unto the Source from whence we came means that we will be wherever God is at all times and in all ways. We will be unlimited in our movements and presence. We shall be as God is, not just simply "up there" but anywhere and everywhere God dwells, at the same time.

A typical sermon at a homegoing service or funeral in many Christian churches includes many of the above-mentioned images. All of the imagery and symbolism of the heavenly realm that John "observed" during his heavenly vision have been woven meticulously and systematically into core beliefs about Heaven by uneducated, misguided, or misinformed preachers and teachers. The same myth has been passed down from one generation of handlers to another to the extent that it has become bedrock in the Christian community, particularly in Black churches. Such songs as "I'll Fly Away," "Deep River," "When We All Get to Heaven," and "Soon as I Get Home" indelibly impress upon the minds of unsuspecting believers that there is a tangible reward awaiting them in the sky "In the Sweet By and By!"

No one would deny that the grieving need something visible and tangible to hold on to, especially at a time of profound loss, to encourage them in their faith walk. Dealing with invisible places and transcendental concepts can unnerve anyone, especially if a person is unsure as to whether or not he or she will gain Heaven after all is said and done. Let's face it, the worry or fear of not going to Heaven after death is more traumatic, troubling, and real than any of us would care to admit.

Yet, Heaven is seldom presented and portrayed as a state of spiritual habitation where the spirit of the invisible God, residing within each person created "in the image and likeness of God" (Gen. 1:26), returns to "the Source from whence it came" (Eccles. 12:7) and becomes as or like God (1 John 3:2). The way Heaven has been presented by countless preachers, teachers, and catechists since time immemorial is a metaphor rather than an actual place of existence.

If Heaven is not a place "in the sweet by and by" with a mansion in the sky, then why strive to be good or do the right thing while on Earth? If every person, bearing the image and likeness of God, will return ultimately to the Source from whence he or she came and become one with God (including even those who may have "fallen short" and must endure a "period of purification"), then why pursue holiness and righteousness in the first place, especially if there is no physical place called *hell*? Why not just do what one wants to do with impunity, never having to worry or weigh the dire consequences of eternal damnation?

The answer lies in the quest for achieving spiritual maturity! Man and woman's ultimate pursuit in life is to reach a level of perfection by reflecting the presence of the invisible God within in visible and tangible ways — in other words, to use one's spiritual energy and time in the flesh to become like God (1 John 3:1–3). The more a person is in divine alignment and synchronization with the Creator, the more that person will be able to manifest the divine traits, characteristics, and attributes that fully reside in God and are seeded in those bearing God's image and likeness, albeit it in a latent or arrested state of development.

The historical Jesus achieved such a divine feat and became God on Earth in fleshly form. He told his followers prior to his earthly departure, "Amen, amen, I say to you, whoever believes in me will do the works that I do, and will do greater ones than these, because I am going to the Father" (John 14:12/NAB). We strive to be righteous, pure, and holy in our daily thoughts, actions, transactions, and reactions in our efforts to reach spiritual perfection. The more we pass through the stages that allowed Jesus to achieve the fullness of divinity, the more we will become a perfect image and reflection of what he actually accomplished in his earthly life:

> In the days when he [Jesus, the Christ] was in the flesh, he offered prayers and supplications with loud cries and tears to the one who was able to save him from death, and he was heard because of his reverence. Son though he was, he learned obedience from what he suffered; and when he was made perfect, he became the source of eternal salvation for all who obey him (Heb. 5:7–9/NAB).

Just as Jesus, the Christ, achieved the fullness of perfection in his earthly life, so are we to accomplish the same. The Gospel of Matthew 5:48 records the challenge Jesus gave to his followers: "So be perfect, just as your heavenly Father is perfect."

When Jesus "was asked by the Pharisees when the kingdom of God would come, he said in reply, 'The coming of the kingdom of God cannot be observed, and no one will announce, "Look, here it is," or "There it is." For behold, the kingdom of God is among you'" (Luke 17:20–21/NAB).

The terms *Kingdom of God* and *Kingdom of Heaven* are used interchangeably by the sacred writers. The Gospel of Matthew prefers the latter usage, whereas the other gospels — Mark, Luke, and John — and the letters of Paul rely more on the former. Various translations say the kingdom is "among you," "within you," or "in your midst." Whatever the expression used, Jesus made it clear that the Kingdom of God or Heaven cannot be seen. It can only be experienced from within, not from without.

The institutionalized Christian church was set on convincing its adherents that the souls of the dearly departed go to "another place" rather than placing emphasis on becoming one with the Source from whence they originally came. Through the utilization of indoctrination and brainwashing, not fidelity to biblical truths, church leaders were able to succeed in cementing the notion that Heaven is a place for the righteous with endless rewards and lavish banquet feasts.

Thus, most Christians have come to believe that, after death, the soul goes to a place of judgment and eternal rest that is beyond the terrestrial sphere. The chasm of physical separation — as in the Parable of the Rich Man and Lazarus (Luke 16:19–31) — is so great that those who remain on Earth feel an urgency to say "goodbye, farewell, or until we meet again." There is little or no sense that, in death, life is changed, not ended. It is very difficult to bring the bereaved to an understanding or acceptance that their loved ones still remain with them, albeit in the form of spirit alone. It is an exhausting task trying to convince or reassure them that the life of their loved one has been transformed completely into a spirit being and that they are now one and the same as God.

The new spiritual transformation means that those who are left behind must begin looking at the lives of those who have preceded them in death in exactly the same manner as they view God. They and God are seamless after death, as they were before coming forth from the Essence of God to take on flesh in their mother's womb. Their lives have come full circle: "As it was in the beginning, is now and ever shall be, world without end. AMEN."

Think for a moment: When was the last time you said to God, "Goodbye, farewell, or until we meet again"? If you have never done so to God, then why do so in regard to someone who has departed? If you believe that they have returned unto God, their Source, then why not see them in the same manner as you see God?

The next time you make the Sign of the Cross, instead of using or saying

61

the habitual formula "In the Name of the Father, and of the Son, and of the Holy Spirit," why not instead say, "I am one with God"? In that way, you will remind yourself each and every day that you are "one with God," not only in earthly life but in eternal life as well.

In the final analysis, Heaven will be viewed and understood from the perspective of a spiritual reunion with God and the holy ancestors rather than a place where one goes to live eternally, moving "to the East Side to a deluxe apartment in the sky," to borrow from the theme song of the *The Jeffersons* sitcom TV series.

The choice is yours: Heaven as a metaphor or Heaven as a state of spiritual existence where "home" is understood as the spirit of God that dwells within you returning and residing in the Essence of God from whence you originally came and, thus, becoming as God has been from the beginning.

CHAPTER 13

Heaven Is Here, There, and Everywhere!

How you deal with death has a direct impact on how you deal with life. The two realities are intertwined and interrelated. In human flesh, life is limited. In the Afterlife, life is forever. While the mortal flesh will die and fade away, the life of God that resides within us will never leave the Earth. Our faith reassures us that it will take on a new form when it is released from the body. Its spiritual movements live eternally and can be here, there, and everywhere at the same time. It will continue to be present in a glorified and unbridled form in a manner that correlates with the oneness of God's ubiquitous nature. It is what I call Heaven.

Heaven is present already within us. It is not a physical place we are seeking but a state of spiritual existence we are striving to fully embrace and achieve each and every day — beginning NOW! It is in our midst, all around us, on top of us and below us, on every corner, next door, in cracks and crevices, in the places where we are, where we've been, and where we are going. YES! Heaven is here, there, and everywhere! Jesus reminded us, "The coming of the kingdom of God [also known as the *Kingdom of Heaven*] cannot be observed, and no one will announce, 'Look, here it is,' or 'There it is.' For behold the kingdom of God is among you" (Luke 17:20–21/NAB).

We should approach every day in a heavenly mindset, with gratitude and appreciation. "Every step we make and every breath we take" should lead us closer to manifesting the presence of the Kingdom of God within us. The kingdom is God's eternal gift to us, and we are its beneficiaries. Even though tomorrow is promised to no one, any moment can be a grace-filled time to seize the day and enjoy life to the fullest. There will be highs and lows, peaks and valleys, successes and trials, sickness and wellness, abundance and want. However, we should never allow any single or isolated moment to deter, distract, or restrict us from taking a long-range approach to life that keeps "Heaven" in view. When life gives you lemons, don't simply make lemonade. Add some strawberries, a splash of ginger ale, and a few mint leaves! Live life to the hilt!

The Word of God reminds us that "eye hath not seen, nor ear heard, neither have entered into the heart of man, the things which God hath prepared for them that love him" (1 Cor. 2:9/KJV). Live with the belief that God loves you with an everlasting love that will never die or fade away. In fact, the love of God only intensifies as we live out life more abundantly in the flesh. We come to realize, through trial and error, how rich and deep is the love that God possesses for us if only we are open and receptive to God's heavenly presence in our lives.

God is not only Creator; God is our Heavenly Parent and relates to us in that manner. Let us start relating to God as a true son or true daughter would relate to his or her earthly parents. God loves us more than we could ever imagine! Human love must attempt to measure up to God's love, not vice versa. The challenge we face each and every day is becoming the agents of God's pure love. We strive to be good, righteous, and holy so that the love of God might be perfected in us. Our lives should abound with the manifestation of God so that others can see the Kingdom of Heaven residing within us. In that way, we become the presence of God on Earth in substantial form. We become as our Elder Brother Jesus, who achieved that feat in his earthly life and became God made man.

Most things in life we can control. Yet, there are things, accompanied by contributing external factors, over which we have no control. In those moments, we need to look within and keep Heaven in our view, reminding ourselves that we came from God, God lives in us, and we will ultimately be victorious and more than conquerors (Rom. 8:37). We will return to be "one with the Source" in all things and in all ways. Yes! We will be here, there, and everywhere God is present!

Many things will occur in the short span of human existence, but we need not be afraid to face the inevitable when the time comes for us to surrender God's life in us back unto God.

There is no need to fear, come what may! "Fear builds its phantoms, which are more fearsome than reality itself," declared Jawaharlal Nehru, the first prime minister of India. "Fear can blind us to the reality in front of us. Yet, we can achieve great things by not letting fear win!"

In the same vein, Sister Carol Myers said, "Our faith reminds us to have no anxiety about the future. For we know with certainty that though the sun sets, it is not gone. It will rise again and, while things appear dormant [in winter], spring will surely come."

Jesus, the Christ, said, "I came so that [you] might have life and have it more abundantly" (John 10:10/NAB). So, do not let the fear of death keep you from living.

Keep Heaven in your view and start experiencing what it must be like to be here, there, and everywhere! After all, God has been doing it ever since time immemorial.

CHAPTER 14

Don't Get Caught Up in the Hype!

If you believe that "Wherever God is, so is Heaven," it logically follows that "Heaven is here, there, and everywhere." Seen in such a light, Heaven as a specified locality should therefore be viewed as a metaphor. Thus, Heaven is not a physical place with material properties capable of being detected by a Global Positioning System (GPS). It is a spiritual state of existence that can be inhabited only by that which is devoid of flesh. Any vision of a place that has anything related to mortal existence or is associated with things pertaining to earthly living cannot be the Kingdom of Heaven. The spirit does not need the things endemic to the body for survival. In the realm of the Spirit, a person is no longer attached to anyone or anything encountered in the sojourn of life on Earth. That's right! No family members, relatives, friends, associates, or enemies. No houses or land, silver or gold, or any other accoutrements, but ONLY those things pertaining to the presence and activity of God! The Scriptures remind us that "flesh and blood cannot inherit the kingdom of God [Kingdom of Heaven], nor does corruption inherit incorruption" (1 Cor. 15:50/NAB).

There are many accounts currently circulating on the internet detailing near-death experiences by those who claim they were on the threshold of entering eternal life. However, in most instances, it was not known why they were sent back to continue their lives in the flesh. In nearly every account of these extraordinary paranormal occurrences, there were certain elements identifiable with physical life that stood out, as recorded in the book 5 *Incredible Stories of Near-Death Experiences*, by Hilary Ribons:

- Those near death were either at the entrance of or "standing in Heaven."
- There was an encounter with or an awareness of a large group of loved ones who had passed on before the near-deceased.
- Material properties, such as an ornate gate, were seen in the "place."
- Many entered through a "tunnel" of glaring and blinding light or were "zooming through a tunnel of pure light."
- There were accounts of "seeing" physical beings, whether Jesus, deceased loved ones, or Jesus holding children in his "arms."
- There were visions of coming "out on the other side in an otherworldly room."
- Some saw an "opened book of moving images."
- One account talked of seeing "three beings [standing] before her, made of giant, shimmering crystal."

However, a word of caution: "Don't get caught up in the hype!" There is more to the story than what meets the eye! The distressed mind can get so caught up in the final moments of physical life that it is only capable of envisioning things with which it is familiar or has experienced on the terrestrial plane. The near-death experience of having purportedly seen a vision of Heaven is colored by a lifetime of teachings about the celestial realm that describe it in terms of physical and material properties. Thus, what is perceived as a "sneak preview" of Heaven is not real.

These personal accounts of near- or actual death experiences all pertain to persons "leaving their body" and finding themselves in another realm. The very fact that the body is "left behind" is a clear indication that flesh and blood cannot inherit (or inhabit) the Kingdom of God/Heaven. "Those who have had near-death experiences say that heaven is unequivocally real — and it is full of unimaginable wonder" (Ribons).

Let us keep in mind that "when it comes to near-death experience stories, there are many unscientific writings based on the writers' own agendas rather than actual evidence. For a near-death experience to occur, one must have limited brain function, yet still have a sensory experience — without full use of their physical senses," this according to "5 Credible Stories of Near Death Experiences," an article written by the Magis Center.

Again, a word of caution: "Don't get caught up in the hype!"

Let us move beyond the accounts of near-death experiences to a consideration of a spiritual occurrence that sometimes takes place with persons who are on the verge of death. The oft-asked question by loved ones and caregivers in those final moments is why the dying appear to be "murmuring" or calling out the names of deceased loved ones just prior to taking their last breath? Are they in a transitional or delirious state of mind while being summoned to join the ranks of the deceased? Are they hallucinating?

A proper understanding or unraveling of this mysterious occurrence begins with the belief that "God is Spirit" (John 4:24). As God stated: "You cannot see my face, for no one may see me and live" (Exod. 33:20/NIV). God, in and of Himself, cannot be known through the utilization of the five senses, especially sight. Yet, we who are the temples of God (1 Cor. 3:16 and 6:19), can best experience the presence of the Godhead when it is manifested in and through each other. When we physically die, the

Word of God states that the breath in us "by which we live, move, and have our being" (Acts 17:28) "returns unto the Source from whence it came" (Eccles. 12:7b)."

Those who have died have been disrobed of their fleshly habitation. The presence of God that dwelt within them has been absorbed and completely enveloped in the fullness of the Essence of their Creator. When our loved ones, standing on the precipice of death, "murmur" or call out the names of those who have preceded them in death, they are envisioning and encountering God in the form of their ancestors, who have taken on the fullness of God's presence. If a believer is looking for a greater reassurance in regard to the existence of the Afterlife, perhaps it can best be found in the experience of dying persons "seeing or communicating" with those who have spiritually ascended. Since they have never "seen" God, God becomes visible through their loved ones who have returned to become one with God. The dying are being welcomed home by their loved ones to "come into the light" and thus become embedded in the same Essence as themselves. In so doing, they become one with them as the spirit people have become one in God. While the above portrayal of an encounter with the Afterlife is unverifiable, it is more plausible than "near-death accounts," since it does not contain any elements associated with the things of Earth.

God is one. All life ebbs and flows from the oneness of this Divine Creative Being and Heavenly Parent. When physical life ends for all of us, we shall return to become one with that same Essence from whence we came in the beginning. When we return unto the Source, we shall possess a divine consciousness that we did not experience in the beginning. What else could it be? As previously mentioned in an earlier chapter, when death casts its dark shadow across our threshold and the spirit of God within our bodies is released, our focus will not be centered on joining our deceased loved ones in a great Family Reunion. It will not be an occasion for catching up on lost time or reliving the good ol' days of yesteryear. It will be about the spirit returning and becoming One with God in the same and exact manner as those who preceded us.

When we engage in an overview of the origins of human life, its presence and purpose on Earth, and its final destiny, we gain a whole new insight into the profound meaning of the Doxology: "Glory be to the Father, and to the Son, and to the Holy Spirit. As it was in the beginning, is now, and ever shall be, world without end. AMEN":

- "As it was in the beginning": when there was only the invisible God.

- "Is now": Our earthly charge NOW is to become one with God by reflecting and manifesting the divine traits, character-istics, and attributes of the invisible God, made visible in us, so that humanity can see and feel God's active presence dwell-ing among us. As the Scriptures state, there is "one Lord, one faith, one baptism, one God and Father of all, who is over all and through all and in all" (Eph. 4:5–6/NAB).

- "And ever shall be": Our ultimate destiny is to return unto that Source from whence we came and become one with God in all things and in all ways.

One final thought: There are not going to be zillions of departed souls "walking around Heaven all day," living in ornate mansions, and enjoying the sumptuous culinary delights of lavish banquet feasts where "the jar of flour shall not go empty, nor the jug of oil run dry" (1 Kings 17:14/NAB). There will be no one "living on the mountain underneath a cloudless sky [or] drinking at the fountain that never shall run dry [or] feasting on the manna from a bountiful supply [while] dwelling in Beulah Land (from "Dwelling In Beulah Land," by Guy Penrod and Jack Toney). Everything and every moment, while we are embedded in God, will be as God has always been from the very beginning, is NOW, and ever shall be, "world without end." Could such a divine awareness give us a hint that this world will never end or be destroyed because, in the final analysis, the Earth shall become God's throne as well as God's footstool?

Now, THAT'S SOMETHING TO GET ALL HYPED UP ABOUT!

CHAPTER 15

Hell? No!

The Eternal Creator God, from whom the essence of all life ebbs and flows, alone knows the final destination of all human beings and how it occurs once they physically die. If one embraces the tenets of traditional teachings promulgated by mainline Christian churches about the Afterlife, the person is made aware that the options are limited. Based on the conduct of a person's life on Earth, those places are Heaven, hell, or somewhere in between.

Beyond the Zoom: The Afterlife is primarily focused on presenting a view and understanding of Heaven as an eternal state of spiritual existence rather than a "place" where the spirit that dwelt within a person goes after physical death to be reunited with God. But what about the existence of hell? if Heaven does not exist as it has been traditionally taught, then what about hell?

Is there actually a place called *hell*, as commonly known, namely, a physical place of eternal suffering and damnation "where the worm does not die, and the fire is not quenched" (Mark 9:48/NAB)? Is it a place of torment, with the material properties of a fiery furnace of brimstone, "where there will be weeping and gnashing of teeth" (Matt. 13:42/NIV)? The answer to this question is: "Hell? No!"

The principal language used to record the Word of God in the Old Testament is Hebrew. The language of the New Testament is Greek, although Jesus spoke in Aramaic. The word *hell* rarely appears in any of the sacred texts. Its character was "inferred from teaching in the biblical texts, some of which, interpreted literally, have given rise to the popular idea of Hell. Theologians today generally see Hell as the logical consequence of rejecting union with God and with God's justice and mercy" ("Hell," *The Oxford Dictionary of the Christian Church*, 2005).

Different Hebrew and Greek words are translated as *hell* in most English-language Bibles. The words most commonly used in the Bible and translated as *hell* are *Sheol, Hades, Gehenna,* and *tartaro.*

Sheol, in the Old Testament and Hades, its New Testament equivalent, are references to *the grave*. "It is generally agreed that both Sheol and Hades do not typically refer to the place of eternal punishment, but to the grave, the temporary abode of the dead, the underworld ("Hell," "Sheol," *New Bible Dictionary*, 3rd edition, InterVarsity Press, 1996).

In Judaism, the word *Gehenna* is employed, which could mean either a place of doom and gloom or a place of purification. In Islam, the word *Barzahk* is used as a place of limbo between paradise and hell.

In the New Testament, Gehenna is described as a place where both soul and body could be destroyed in unquenchable fire. When Jesus applied the analogy of the fires of Gehenna as a place for wicked and evil persons, he was speaking of a physical location outside the walls of Jerusalem, where trash and dung were taken and burned, not of hell as most Christians have come to believe. The site was also an isolated gathering place for lepers and outcasts to languish — thus the expression "weeping and gnashing of teeth."

Jesus spoke often in ambiguous language. On the one hand, he spoke of Gehenna on several occasions as a place of "unquenchable fire" reserved for those who at the end of their lives refused to believe and be converted, where both body and soul can be lost. Jesus, known for his facile usage of hyperbolic and parabolic expressions, such as "plucking out an eye" or "cutting off a limb," used every means at his disposal to remind his followers of the need to repent and be saved to avoid a catastrophic end.

Yet, on the other hand, Jesus spoke of God's tender love and mercy, saying, for example, "for [God] himself is kind to the ungrateful and the wicked. Be merciful, just as [also] your Father is merciful" (Luke 6:35b–36/NAB).

In the Parable of the Rich Man and Lazarus, an account particular only to the Gospel of Luke (16:19–26/NAB), Jesus spoke of the rich man being in torment in the "nether world" for refusing to come to the aid of poor Lazarus by providing him food from his sumptuous table. When Lazarus died, the story says,

> he was carried away by angels to the bosom of Abraham [where Abraham was exactly, is never mentioned!]. The rich man also died and was buried, and from the nether world, where he was in torment, he raised his eyes and saw Abraham far off and Lazarus at his side. And he cried out, "Father Abraham, have pity on me. Send Lazarus to dip the tip of his finger in water and cool my tongue, for I am suffering torment in these flames." Abraham replied, "My child, remember that you received what was good during your lifetime while Lazarus likewise received what was bad; but now he is comforted here, whereas you are tormented. Moreover, between us and you a great chasm is established to prevent anyone from crossing who might wish to go from our side to yours or from your side to ours."

This Gospel selection is perhaps the only concrete example in all of Scripture where Jesus suggests a specific place of eternal damnation. But remember, it was only a parable! And parables were meant to teach a lesson, not to establish doctrine.

Tartaro, a Greek verb that appears only once in the New Testament (2 Pet. 2:4) is almost always translated by a phrase such as *thrown down to hell*, in reference to the root meaning of the word having to do with a subterranean place of divine punishment lower than Hades.

A couple of noted sayings of Jesus utilized by church authorities to advance the doctrine of hell are found in the Gospel of Matthew: "Depart from me, you accursed, into the eternal fire prepared for the devil and his angels" (Matt. 25:11/NAB) and "The Son of Man will send his angels, and they will collect out of his kingdom all who cause others to sin and all evildoers. They will throw them into the fiery furnace, where there will be wailing and grinding of teeth" (Matt. 13:41–42/NAB).

Hell ranks in the category of allegorical literature and did not reach its prominence until centuries later when such poets as Dante Alighieri and John Milton envisioned hell as a place of physical torment and mass destruction. And that is exactly where the so-called doctrine on hell should remain: within the annals of great literature and not employed as a fear factor in scaring the hell out of people.

Hell, like Heaven, is not a physical place but a state of spiritual existence. Pope John Paul II, the late spiritual leader of the Roman Catholic Church (recently declared to be a saint), stated in a decree on July 28, 1999, in speaking of hell as a place, "The Bible uses 'a symbolic language,' which must be correctly interpreted. ... Rather than a place, hell indicates the state of those who freely and definitively separate themselves from God, the source of all life and joy." The *Catholic Faith Handbook for Youth* (Saint

Mary's Press, p. 421) says that, "more accurately, heaven and hell are not places but states [of existence]."

Yet, there are many faith traditions that tenaciously hold to the belief that hell is actually a physical place of eternal damnation where the spirit of an evil or deadly sinful person languishes in a pit of unquenchable fire.

To unravel the truth about hell, the believer must first ask the question: "What part of a deceased person — his soul or his body — would be sentenced to hell if it were found to be displeasing to God and deserving of eternal damnation?" Religion teaches that it is the soul that will stand in judgment, not the body. Just as flesh and blood cannot inherit the Kingdom of God (Kingdom of Heaven) (1 Cor. 15:50), neither can flesh and blood inherit hell. It is another concrete example of how institutionalized religion has engaged in scare tactics in an effort to control the masses.

If it is the corrupt soul, not the body, that is purportedly damned and sentenced to hell, then how does one explain "weeping and gnashing of teeth" when there is no flesh that accompanies the soul to judgment? No flesh means no eyes to weep or teeth to gnash! The spirit cannot be burned, destroyed, or subjugated to physical properties because it is above and beyond the physical plane.

In essence, hierarchical religious leaders have lied to their adherents about the existence of hell as a place of eternal damnation. It is not biblically sound, nor can the Word of God be manipulated and twisted to justify or substantiate its existence. In the words of Malcolm X, folks in the pew have been "had, fooled, hoodwinked, and bamboozled" by their so-called religious leaders.

The Book of Genesis records that man and woman were created in the divine image and likeness of God (Gen. 1:26). The totality of the nature or Essence of God is Spirit (John 4:24), not flesh. Therefore, that which bears God's image and likeness is solely in the realm of spirit, not flesh. It is likewise recorded in Genesis 2:7 that God, the Creator, scooped up dirt from the Earth, shaped it into a corporeal mass, and then breathed into it the breath of Life, causing man to become a living soul/being.

The essence of life is contained solely in the spiritual nature of man and woman. The spirit does not need the body in order to exist (see the Book of Ezekiel, chapter 37). However, the body is as good as dead if there is no spirit, or breath, dwelling within it. That which lives on after physical death is the breath, or soul.

If the body is of the Earth and the spirit that makes man and woman live, move, and have their being (Acts 17:28) is of God, how then can that which expires be condemned to hell if the breath not only originates from God but is the very essence of God Himself? The burning question then is, "Can God be condemned to hell?" What answer do the astute and erudite theologians and the manipulators of the truth have in regard to that issue? You either believe that every human being has divinity residing within him- or herself, which is the essence of God, or that the whole concept of being made in the image and likeness of God is an exercise in sophistry.

If the soul is that which either merits Heaven or deserves hell upon death, as taught by traditional belief systems, then what answer does one provide to the following question: "If every human being received life from the breath of God being blown into the corporeal mass in his or her mother's womb, then how can there be a condemnation or sentencing to hell of that spirit if it is the essence of God?" Every person born in the flesh bears the invisible spirit of the living God (Gen. 1:26), and without that presence of God within, there is no life!

One could argue that there is a physical hell, but not in the manner in which it has been traditionally taught. In the words of the Honorable

Minister Elijah Muhammad, the Messenger of God of the Nation of Islam, "Both heaven and hell are conditions of life on earth." Heaven is here — it is in our midst, it is within us (Luke 17:20–21) — and so is hell. Hell is here on Earth. It is not "below" somewhere.

In contrast, the fullness of Heaven can be experienced only after the spirit is released from the physical confines of the body. And man and woman cannot be fully released from hell on Earth until the spirit that comes from within has been purified and is ready to return to the Source.

Yet, the pressing and unresolved question still remains: "How can the spirit of God that resides within every human being and is the essence of life itself be sentenced to hell once it leaves the mortal confines of the body?" The central issue is not whether a person died in sin so as to deserve hell. It is whether the mercy of God intersects the plight of the spirit's ascent before judgment and absolves it eventually of its transgressions.

Many religions of the world understood this spiritual dilemma without admitting to the rationale behind creating a means for the soul or spirit to be purified before returning to the Source from whence it came. An examination of the various teachings of the principal Abrahamic faiths contains a belief about a "holding stage" or a period of cleansing after death before the soul or spirit reaches perfection. *Purgatory*, which is related to purgation or cleansing, is a major tenet of belief in the Roman Catholic Church. Even though there is no mention of a place called *purgatory* in the Bible, the Roman Catholic Church has been steadfast in holding to a belief in its existence. Other Christian religions reject the stance, claiming that the act of people being cleansed of their sins defeats the purpose of Jesus's sacrifice on Calvary.

Regardless of the paucity of passages in the Bible that deal with hell or its derivatives as places of eternal damnation, with physical properties, they are implausible and incompatible with the biblical declarations pertaining to the nature of spirit that resides within man and woman and where that spirit goes once it leaves the body and returns unto the Source from whence it came. The spirit is the essence of God within each of us. There is no life apart from it. When the spirit is released from the body at the moment of physical death, it lives in the fullness of the Spirit of God. Life resides solely in the spirit, and it is that spirit that makes the body "live, move, and have its being" (Acts 17:28). If that which is in man and woman returns unto God, it is the essence of the Godhead. The body is buried or cremated. The spirit reunites once again with its Creator.

It is not the body that stands in judgment before God. It is the Spirit of God Himself that dwelled in human flesh. Can God judge God? Can God be separated from life? Can that which is of the very nature of God be condemned and sentenced to eternal damnation?

Hell? No!

CHAPTER 16

When Bad People Die

If hell does not exist, then what happens to bad people when they die? What happens to the spirit that dwelt in them that allowed them to "live, move, and have their being?" (Acts 17:28). Where does it go? It, too, will eventually return to the Source from whence it came (Eccles. 12:7b). But how is it so?

The basis for stating that hell does not exist as traditionally presented by mainline Christianity and, in particular, by conservative and fundamentalist religion is due to the belief that that which makes human beings live, move, and have their being is the spirit of the invisible God dwelling within them. When the breath expires and leaves the body, it "returns unto the Source from whence it came." The body is either buried or cremated, thus returning to the earth from whence it came (Eccles. 12:7a).

If the sole element within human beings that conveys life is the spirit or breath of God's presence, then how can the essence of God, once it leaves the body, be condemned or sentenced to hell? God is Pure Spirit (John 4:24), and that which remains after a person's death is pure spirit. Thus, every human being created in "the image and likeness" of God (Gen. 1:26) ultimately will return to become one with the Source.

An understanding of the biblical treatise as presented above still does not resolve the issue of where bad people go after they die. There is no question in the mind of a traditional believer that such a theological stance is seriously untenable and unacceptable as well as deeply troubling and disturbing for the masses of people who are doing their darndest to live an upright and holy life. Why should those who have lived decadent and evil lives deserve to be rewarded with an eternal life of peace and joy? After all, did they not deserve to be sentenced to the lowest depths of hell as eternal payment for their earthly dastardly deeds? How could a just God allow them to dwell in the company of good people who consistently sacrificed and denied themselves from engaging in all the sordid, damnable things in life?

Some believers might even retort by referring to the New Testament passage uttered by Jesus: "Truly I tell you, you will not get out until you have paid the last penny" (Matt. 5:26/NIV). Jesus had a penchant for utilizing hyperbolic expressions to get across a point, such as plucking out an eye or cutting off a limb (Matt. 5:29–30). However, even in this exaggerated citation of paying the last penny, it pertains to getting out of prison, not getting out of hell.

While there may be no conclusive or justifiable reason as to why bad and "rotten to the core" evil persons eventually will end up in the same state of existence as righteous people after physical death, no one can stand in God's position when it comes to passing judgment. God's thoughts are not our thoughts and God's ways are not our ways (Isa. 55:8). The Bible clearly states, "For who knows a person's thoughts except their own spirit within them? In the same way no one knows the thoughts of God except the Spirit of God" (1 Cor. 2:11/NIV). Another biblical passage leaning in the same direction says, "How unsearchable are his judgments and how inscrutable his ways! 'For who has known the mind of the Lord, or who has been his counselor?' 'Or who has given a gift to him that he might be repaid?' For from him and through him and to him are all things" (Rom. 11:33-36).

Let us never forget that God, our Creator and Heavenly Parent, is more kind, merciful, gentle, and compassionate than the human mind can comprehend. For God to lose any person to eternal damnation would be like losing a part of Himself or His spiritual child who is the embodiment of Himself.

"The Lord does not delay [as though He were unable to act] and is not slow about His promise, as some count slowness, but is [extraordinarily] patient toward you, not wishing for any to perish but for all to come to repentance" (2 Pet. 3:9/AMP).

Consider this passage where the Lord declares, "Do I take any pleasure in the death of the wicked? Rather, am I not pleased when they turn from their ways and live?" (Ezek. 18:23/NIV).

There can be no excuse or justification for evil and those who are caught in its snare. Repentance is required by a person turning away from their wicked ways and engaging in some form of indemnity as restitution for past transgressions.

Indemnity is defined as 1) protection or security against damage or loss, 2) compensation for damage or loss sustained, 3) something paid by way of such compensation, or 4) protection, as by insurance, from liabilities or penalties incurred by one's actions (Wikipedia).

Indemnity must be paid either directly by the individual during their earthly life or by generations to come who will bear the burden and carry the guilt of their forebearers' sins,

"You shall not worship them or serve them; for I, the Lord your God, am a jealous (impassioned) God [demanding what is rightfully and uniquely mine], visiting (avenging) the iniquity (sin, guilt) of the fathers on the children [that is, calling the children to account for the sins of their fathers], to the third and the fourth generations of those who hate Me, but showing graciousness and lovingkindness to thousands [of generations] of those who love Me and keep My commandments" (Deut. 5:9–10/AMP).

The ancient believers listed in the Bible who died without seeing the fulfillment of the Promise were able to be beneficiaries and sharers of what was to come through the righteous works of their descendants: "Yet all these, though approved because of their faith, did not receive what has been promised. God had foreseen something better for us, so that without us they should not be made perfect" (Heb. 11:39–40/NAB).

Could a similar situation apply to evil persons (or even those who simply "fell short") who died without being purified so as to return immediately to the Source from whence they came? Is there a price that their descendants must pay as compensation for their ancestors' heinous or simply selfish transgressions? Will tragedy and misfortune occur in their lives and in the lives of their children and grandchildren, not as a result of anything that they did personally but as restitution for the sins of their forebearers? Could it be as a consequence of a "generational curse" initiated by the ancestors who lived evil or imperfect lives?

If generational indemnity on behalf of their deceased loved ones can purify the souls of the wicked to return to the Source, then what is the purpose of even striving to do what is good or what the Lord requires of us, such as "acting justly, loving mercy and walking humbly with our God?" (Mic. 6:8). Why not join the club and be and do like the rest of sinful humanity?

Man and woman were created in the "image and likeness" of God to become, first and foremost, the visible and tangible manifestation of the invisible God on Earth. Such a level could only be reached by human beings spiritually growing and perfecting themselves in a similar pattern as Jesus, our Elder Brother, accomplished during his physical time on Earth. In his lifetime, He became fully God and fully man.

The Scriptures point to this progression of spiritual maturation in Jesus's life as well as in the lives of those called to follow him: "In the days when he [Jesus] was in the flesh, he offered prayers and supplications with loud cries and tears to the one who was able to save him from death, and he was heard because of his reverence. Son though he was, he learned obedience from what he suffered; and when he was made perfect, he became the source of eternal salvation for all who obey him" (Heb. 5:7–9/NAB).

Jesus boldly declared to his followers, "Be perfect, therefore, as your heavenly Father is perfect" (Matt. 5:48). Perfection comes through spiritual growth and development by denying oneself, taking up one's cross daily, and following in the footsteps of Jesus, the Master Teacher (Luke 9:23). Only then will a person be able to do all things (Matt. 17:20) through faith. Human beings, in and of themselves, will run into the impossible at every turn. However, with God in man, all things are possible (Matt. 19:26).

The spiritual end of each person is to become "like or as" God is: "Beloved, now we are children of God, and it has not appeared as yet what we will be. We know that when He appears, we will be like Him, because we will see Him just as He is" (1 John 3:2/NAB).

Thus, we as believers, strive to be holy and righteous so that we can "unlock" the treasures to the Kingdom of Heaven (Matt. 6:19–34) and the manifold wisdom of God (Eph. 3:10). It is not about eschewing evil so that we can gain Heaven after we physically die but more about spiritually growing and maturing so that we can become God's substantial presence on Earth.

Perhaps, if church authorities focused more on developing the spirituality of their adherents in terms of discovering and actualizing their real identity, purpose, and destiny in life rather than forcing them into a religious peg hole that binds them to doctrine and tradition, more believers would seek spiritual perfection as a prelude to unleashing the power of the Godhead within. Then, and only then, could they unite together to establish the Kingdom of God on Earth.

The believer does not have time to be preoccupied with what happens when bad people die. Perhaps that is what Jesus meant when he said, "Let the dead bury the dead" (Matt. 8:28/NAB). Our focus should be on "seek[ing] first the Kingdom of God and His righteousness" (Matt. 6:33/NAB). Do not worry about what will happen eventually to bad people. As humans, we are so quick to judge and sentence others to hell without giving them the benefit of the doubt or weighing their transgressions against our own unworthiness.

"Do not worry about tomorrow; tomorrow will take care of itself. Sufficient for a day is its own evil" (Matt. 6:34/NAB).

CHAPTER 17

Preparing for Death

Can you prepare for death? It may sound like an odd or disturbing question, but anything with eternality in it deserves serious thought, consideration, and long-range preparation. After all, who gets ready to go on a trip or a vacation of a lifetime without proper planning, anticipating everything that is required to make it an unforgettable and lasting experience? Why wouldn't you want to give greater priority, meaning, and importance to that which will last for an eternity?

The Book of Ecclesiastes reminds us that "to every thing there is a season, and a time to every purpose under the heaven; a time to be born and a time to die" (Eccles. 3:1–2/KJV).

Since we know that "it is appointed unto man to die once" (Heb. 9:27/ KJV), then how does a person prepare himself for the inevitable? If the Zoom Effect is so minuscule in comparison to the Afterlife, then we should never allow the latter to be so far removed from our view that we think this life is all that exists. One doesn't have to be preoccupied or obsessed with death to the extent that it affects a person's quality of living. However, it must be kept in proper perspective. What bears more importance to you: a physical life span of seventy, eighty, or a hundred years on earth in the flesh or the fullness of a ubiquitous life that will never end?

Yes, all of us are going to physically die. While such a statement is self-evident because of what we have witnessed in human history, the manner in which we face the reality of our own mortal demise varies and greatly depends on the depths of our faith. We ask ourselves: "When, how, or in what manner will our own death occur?" The exactitude of that moment is known to the Creator alone. Our striving should be focused on aligning and synchronizing our lives with the will and purpose of the One who breathed us into existence. As we move closer and closer to achieving a level of divine harmony and oneness with God, we will discover that not only can we enjoy life on Earth but we can live it more abundantly.

People used to say there are only two things a person cannot avoid in life: death and taxes! I am not so sure about the latter but about the former I am most assuredly certain! Since you and I cannot avoid death, we might as well learn how to live with it so that when the inevitable happens, we will not be caught off guard but be ready to embrace it.

I hardly know of anyone who is remotely excited about even the thought of dying, no less death itself, including this author. No matter how often I have tried to imagine myself lying in a state of peaceful repose, with those left behind being transfixed and lovingly gazing upon my mortal remains, I cannot even begin to fathom what that moment of spiritual ascension will bring with it. This life is all that we know, even though most of us are not even at the point of figuring it out or mastering it. We are deeply afraid and terrified of any thought of an afterlife over which we ultimately have no control. We cannot cope with someone else calling the shots or dictating the terms of our final destination.

But death is what it is, and there's no getting around it! It is the Great Equalizer, reducing all of us to the same state of existence. No person has the power to control or change it except the One who has called us all into being.

If we had our druthers, we would readily and hastily choose not to die, even in the face of the complexities and vicissitudes of life. Some of us would prefer poverty or a debilitating sickness rather than yielding to the forces of death that, ironically, initiate the process of perpetual health. Better to deal with things with which we are familiar than encounter the uncertainties of the unknown.

- Death haunts us, especially when confronted with the whens and hows of its nature. When will we die: in the prime of life or at a ripe old age? Even more so, how will it occur or manifest itself? Will it be in the throes of sleep or as a result of a terminal illness, vehicular accident, drowning, suicide, fratricide, homicide, road rage, plane crash, accidental shooting, freak accident, a nuclear destruction, or war? What are we more preoccupied or concerned about: "THE WHEN OR THE HOW?"

- But why even be obsessed about it? Death will probably visit us at a time when we least expect it. There is no such thing as the right time to die or dying before one's time. Whenever death strikes or comes for each of us, that's our time! There is no need to become all absorbed in the nuances of death. Who can figure it out in the first place? If anything, we ought to focus on preparing to die in order to live!

- To live is to die, and to die is to live! The apostle Paul said, "For to me, to live is Christ and to die is gain" (Phil. 1:21/NIV). It was not that the apostle was absorbed with a life of doom and gloom. He was more focused on human life's ultimate end.

Let's face it: The Afterlife is not a favorite subject! Making it from day to day extracts enough energy to drain us. We can barely place one foot in front of the other, no less contemplate what life must be like "walking on streets paved with gold." Besides, daily thoughts of personally dying can drive any sane person insane and into a state of depression. So, live the best of your life NOW! Leave all worries behind that prevent you from living a more abundant life. Do not worry about tomorrow; today has enough cares of its own (Matt. 6:34/NAB).

The following thoughts are offered as a means of putting life and death in their proper perspective so as to develop the right frame of mind in properly preparing for death:

- Life is a dress rehearsal for eternity.
- We need to come to terms with our finiteness.
- Our mortal flesh will not live forever.
- The only way we could have avoided death was to never have been born.
- The first step in easing the stress of death is getting a grip on the fear of death itself.
- Why fear that which is going to befall everyone born of mortal flesh?
- Why be afraid of dying when there is absolutely nothing a person can do about it?
- As the saying goes, "You can run [from death] but you cannot hide."
- When all is said and done, it's about "letting go and letting God" take control.

In the midst of "letting go and letting God," there is nothing to fear. Has anything positive ever been accomplished in life by fearing something over which we have no control? To reiterate, life is a dress rehearsal for eternity. The first thing we need to resolve in our mind is how to embrace and relate to our finiteness. Our mortal flesh will not live forever. The only way to avoid such an undertaking is never to have been born! Since that is not the case for any of us, the first step in easing the stress of death is getting a grip on the fear of death itself. Why fear what is going to befall each of us? Why be afraid of death when there is absolutely nothing a person can do to avoid it? As the saying goes, "You can run [from death] but you cannot hide."

Fear is not going to remove death from our doorstep. In fact, it is still couching at our door! The thirty-second president of the United States, Franklin Delano Roosevelt, stated without equivocation, "We have nothing to fear but fear itself." We must simply learn how to deal with fear before it deals with us. We are all going to have to take the final journey alone one day. No one will be standing there along the way cheering us on or pushing us toward the finish line. It's each man for himself and God for us all.

We fear that which we do not know. Let's face it. Life on Earth is our comfort zone, like Linus's blanket in the cartoon strip *Peanuts*. Our lives may be tumultuous, but clinging to life is our "Linus blanket," providing a sense of warmth, security, and comfort in the midst of a troubled and unsettled world. This life is all we know. No matter how miserable or disturbing life may be or the seemingly unsurmountable trials and tribulations that confront us each and every day, we would rather endure life's "slings and arrows of outrageous misfortune" (*Hamlet*, Act III, Scene I) than face the uncertainties that await us beyond the grave.

If there is any consolation or encouragement in conquering the fear of death, the Word of God reminds us in the Old Testament deuterocanonical Book of Wisdom that "the souls of the just are in the hand of God, and no torment shall touch them. They seemed, in the view of the foolish, to be dead; and their passing away was thought an affliction and their going forth from us, utter destruction. But they are in peace" (Ws 3:1–3/NAB).

In the New Testament, the Word of God states that those of us who remain on Earth in no way have an advantage over those who have fallen asleep (1 Thess. 4:15).

No one living in the flesh knows with absolute certainty what life will consist of when we return unto the Source from whence we came and become one with that Divine Entity. However, the Word of God reassures us that we shall possess the exact nature and divine consciousness of God (1 John 3:2). How we will take on the fullness of God and become like unto God is the greatest mystery of all time. It is the last piece of the puzzle to be put into place. Only when we return to our Source will it be completely known, namely, what it is to be like or as God and possessing the mind of God. All we can say is that, if God is omnipotent, then we shall be omnipotent; if God is omniscient, then we shall be omniscient; if God is omnipresent and ubiquitous, then we, too, shall be omnipresent and ubiquitous. As the apostle Paul reminds us:

"Oh, the depth of the riches and wisdom and knowledge of God! How inscrutable are his judgments and how unsearchable his ways! 'For who has known the mind of the Lord or who has been his counselor?'" (Rom. 11:33–34/NAB).

Once we move beyond the fear of death, we can embark on the process of growing spiritually by being "transformed by the renewal of our mind" (Rom. 12:2/NAB). We must reconstruct our mind to "see" as God sees and strive to be in compliance with what God expects of us to inherit eternal life.

The Word of God is "a lamp unto our feet and a light unto our path" (Ps. 119:105) in achieving the goal of taking the Second Step and preparing ourselves for physical death. We must strive to obey and apply the Word of God in all our thoughts, actions, dealings, and undertakings with others, who are likewise temple branches where the invisible God resides. When asked about which commandment in the law was the greatest, Jesus said:

"'You shall love the Lord your God with all your heart, and with all your soul, and with all your mind.' This is the greatest and first commandment. And a second is like it: 'You shall love your neighbor as yourself.' All the Law and the Prophets hang on these two commandments" (Matt. 22:37–40).

There is no getting around it! The Greatest Commandment is both vertical and horizontal. It must manifest itself on both levels: a love for God and a love for one another. You cannot have one without the other. Both are required to make love authentic.

In the First Letter of John 4:19–21/NAB, the Word of God explicitly states, "We love because He [God, the Source/Creator] first loved us. If anyone says, 'I love God,' but hates his brother, he is a liar; for whoever does not love a brother whom he has seen cannot love God whom he has not seen. This is the commandment we have from him: whoever loves God must also love his brother."

How often over the centuries have humanity and religion, especially its hierarchical leaders, misread, misrepresented, or misinterpreted the above stringent passages? As a result of spiritual negligence, they gave license to that which permitted racism, discrimination, segregation, and prejudice "to fester like a sore, and then run, stinking like rotten meat, or crust and sugar over — like a syrupy sweet" (paraphrase of the poem "Harlem," by Langston Hughes).

Sometimes, people act like they don't know better, but in reality they do! Religious leaders have often been spineless, bowing down to social, political, financial, and institutional pressures residing in principalities and powers, with the world rulers of darkness and with evil spirits in the heavens (Eph. 6:12). They claim to represent God, but actually are "noisy gongs and clashing cymbals."

The Word of God tells us what is the right thing to do: "You have been told, O man, what is good, and what the Lord requires of you: Only to do the right [thing] and love goodness, and to walk humbly with your God" (Mic. 6:8/NAB).

The great Early Church Father Saint Augustine of Hippo, in his "Love Sermon," said, "Love and do what you will." If our love is genuine, sincere, and rooted in God's love, then we need not be preoccupied with crossing every "t" and dotting every "i." All of our thoughts, words, deeds, habits, and character will be tempered by our relationship with God.

Last, let our lives be governed by the Golden Rule and the Divine Mandate. The sayings, deeds, and actions of the Old Testament are summarized in a single statement: "Do to others whatever you would have them do to you." Jesus, the Christ, said, "This is the Law and the Prophets" (Matt. 7:12/NAB).

"The Golden Rule is the principle of treating others as one wants to be treated. It is a maxim that is found in most religions and cultures. It can be considered an ethic of reciprocity in some religions, although different religions treat it differently" ("Golden Rule," Wikipedia)."

In prayer, fasting, and giving of our substance (traditionally known as *almsgiving*), we come to clearly understand our relation to God and to one another and what is required of us as agents of God. We are able to demonstrate our divine alignment with God and acknowledge that everything we possess is a pure gift of God. It is not meant solely for ourselves but to be used in accomplishing the divine mission for which we were born into this world.

The Divine Mandate gives articulation and meaning to what it means to "live for the sake of others" (Sun Myung Moon, founder of the Holy Spirit Association for the Unification of World Christianity) and to truly love others as we purport to love God. Jesus, the Master Teacher, talked about the end times:

> When the Son of Man comes in his glory, and all the angels with him, he will sit upon his glorious throne, and all the nations will be assembled before him. And he will separate them one from another, as a shepherd separates the sheep from the goats. He will place the sheep on his right and the goats on his left. Then the king will say to those on his right, "Come, you who are blessed by my Father. Inherit the kingdom prepared for you from the foundation of the world. For I was hungry and you gave me food, I was thirsty and you gave me drink, a stranger and you welcomed me, naked and you clothed me, ill and you cared for me, in prison and you visited me." Then the righteous will answer him and say, "Lord, when did we see you hungry and feed you, or thirsty and give you drink? When did we see you a stranger and welcome you, or naked and clothe you? When did we see you ill or in prison and visit you?" And the king will say to them in reply, "Amen, I say to you, whatever you did for one of these least brothers of mine, you did for me" (Matt. 25:31–40/NAB).

In summation, if we can incorporate into our daily living the divine plan that God has given for everyday living, we will have done all that God requires of us to possess eternal life. In preparing for death, we will have no fear of what is to come. As the saying goes, "Don't sweat the small stuff." You can avoid all of the nitpicking in your life. Besides, doing so is nothing more than a distraction that will take you off course.

When death comes, realize that it is only a pause in life, not an end. The journey continues. Death may be called the *Great Interrupter*, but when it fizzles out, it will have lost the battle. As the Scriptures state, "And when this which is corruptible clothes itself with immortality, then the word that is written shall come about: 'Death is swallowed up in victory. Where, O death, is your victory? Where, O death, is your sting?'" (1 Cor. 15:54–55/NAB).

Remember, death is out of your control, and there is absolutely nothing you can do to avoid it. Leave the "small stuff" to God.

Let us live each day as if it were the first, last, and only day of our life so that when the inevitable moment arrives and this world can afford us a home no longer, we can return to the Source from whence we came without any regrets and live life anew forever in God.

Death will have its day in every life. Yet, it will not claim the victory over us if we keep it in proper perspective by preparing for death, which leads to everlasting life!

CHAPTER 18

Keep Death in Your Rearview Mirror

Dealing with inconsolable grief caused by the physical death of those whom we have loved and lost can oftentimes be too much for the human heart to bear. Accepting the reality that they are no longer physically present in our midst seems unimaginable. We ask ourselves how it is possible to adjust to their passing when so much of our individual world centered around our interaction and involvement with them. Why did they have to go and we be left behind? How can we find the strength to keep on keeping on without them?

All these questions and more haunt us at the time of a person's death. While we know that death is inevitable and that there is an appointed time (Eccles. 3:1 and Heb. 9:27) for each of us to physically transition, most of us are never ready to embrace it, even though there may be signs and indications that death is imminent. We seem to have no desire to focus or concentrate on things that are disturbing, disruptive, or unpleasant in daily living.

None of us should be so obsessed with death that we allow it to become our primary preoccupation or concern. At the same time, we should never live in such a way that we forget that death is ever present in our midst. One day, our time will come, and we will reach the cashier at the end of the checkout line. While the song says "I've Got Heaven in My View," just remember it might not be a bad idea to "Keep Death in Your Rearview Mirror" as well.

The purpose of a rearview mirror is to allow a driver to view what is behind him without having to turn his head in an awkward fashion. One's primary focus while driving is on what lies ahead and on reaching one's destination, not on what is behind the driver. But the rearview mirror serves as an indispensable instrument to inform the driver if another vehicle or object is encroaching or is close behind the driver's vehicle that could endanger or impede its operation or performance.

There is no such thing as having death sneak or creep up on you if you keep it in its proper perspective. Nothing can ever surprise you if it is anticipated or expected. The best thing is to be properly prepared for it. Most people are thrown for a loop when death strikes, especially if it occurs suddenly, even though they know that it is part and parcel of life itself. How many times have we heard the third chapter, verse 1, of the Book of Ecclesiastes quoted by preacher and layperson alike: "A time to be born and a time to die."

As a people, we cry tears of joy when a new life is born into the world, yet with those same eyes we cry tears of sorrow at the physical passing of a loved one. Shouldn't it be just the opposite? What that newborn baby will encounter in the world as we currently know it should cause any of us to weep. Knowing that our loved one has overcome the powers of death, hell, sin, and the grave in physical death should cause all of us to shed tears of joy!

Keeping death in your rearview mirror allows you to keep moving forward to your eternal destination while on the lookout for anything behind you that might hinder or endanger your well-being or progress in living a more abundant life. Let not even the reality of death prevent you from living life to the fullest. Live each day of this beautiful life that our God has bequeathed to and bestowed upon you as if it were your first, last, and only day so that, when the hour of death comes, you will have no regrets! Fear not that over which you have no control. Keep moving forward with a zeal and a zest for life while, at the same time, reassuring yourself that even though you do not have control or the ability to prevent death from occurring, it will mark the beginning of a new life for you when it does occur.

Keep death in your rearview mirror, not in front of you, as you continue moving forward to living a more abundant life.

CHAPTER 19

"Let Go and Let God"

How often has the expression been uttered: "Let go and let God"? When facing the reality of death, no words could be more comforting or reassuring. There comes a point in life when all of us have to release ourselves from a preoccupation with those things over which we have no ultimate control. We must put our trust in God, even as we stand on the threshold of death. Our God will neither forsake us nor abandon us. As the song says, "[We are] not forgotten. God knows [our] name!"

What is to be gained by avoiding a perennial issue that has eternal consequences? Why fight or resist the inevitable? After all, death is nothing new to any of us. We have all been present at a funeral before and we will be present again and again until it comes our turn for others to be present for us! The experience of the death of a loved one is not our first time at the rodeo!

The mindset that we possess about life, death, and eternal life will determine the manner by which we face and come to grips with the reality of our own existence, whether temporary or eternal. No one knows the day or hour when death will cast its dark shadow across our pathway.

There is no question about it. If given the choice, each of us would prefer to set the terms as to when, where, how, and under what circumstances our death will occur. But that cannot be granted to any of us, because it is not our right to choose the day or the hour. Jesus's statement in the Gospel of Matthew about the end times applies likewise to the end time for each of us personally: "But about that day or hour no one knows, not even the angels in heaven, nor the Son, but only the Father" (Matt. 24:36/NIV).

For most of us, death will come when we least expect it, without our affairs in order, and at the most inopportune time for those left behind who need to ready themselves for our physical demise. After all, there is no perfect time to die!

For the believer, the only reassurance of life after death is embedded in the Word of God. As the apostle Paul stated, "For to me, to live is Christ and to die is gain" (Phil. 1:21/NAB). Paul realized that whether he lived or died, he would still be a winner! In the final analysis, he realized that there was something more to be gained by dying than remaining permanently in the flesh: "We are confident, I say, and willing rather to be absent from the body, and to be present with the Lord" (2 Cor. 5:8/KJV).

A metaphysical approach to life after death is required to understand that there is nothing to fear in dying. Man and woman are more than brain and blood, sinew, skin, and flesh. They are spiritual beings robed or clothed in flesh with a life span that is eternal, not temporary. Death is only the gateway to a life that will know no end. When the invisible spirit of God within us completes its final cycle, all things will be made new.

The only fight in which we need to engage is the one the apostle Paul spoke of when undertaking a self-examination and assessment of his life in the flesh: "I have fought the good fight, I have finished the race, I have kept the faith. Now there is in store for me the crown of righteousness, which the Lord, the righteous Judge, will award to me on that day — and not only to me, but also to all who have longed for his appearing" (2 Tim. 4:7–8/NIV).

The only thing we need to resist is "the devil, and he will flee from [us]" (James 4:7/KJV). If we submit ourselves to God, when the inevitable comes, we will be safe and secure from all alarm in God's arms.

It is time for us to incorporate into our everyday living the practice of "letting go and letting God" by freeing ourselves from all anxiety and fear of dying. Our ultimate hope and trust rest in God. In that way, we will not fight or resist the inevitability of physical death but embrace it when the appointed hour arrives for each and every one of us in due season.

CHAPTER 20

Get Ready for
the Great Release!

And the dust returns to the earth as it once was,

and the life breath returns to God who gave it.

— Eccles. 12:7/NAB

Before there was a beginning, if such a thing could ever be imagined, Spirit existed in its primordial form as eternal and boundless, with nothing that could contain, limit, or hold It. All things ebbed and flowed from this creative Spirit Being. Life in the flesh that man and woman would eventually experience came as a result of being formed "in the image and likeness of God" (Gen. 1:26). Life itself pertains to the spirit realm that contains the divine or spiritual traits, characteristics, and attributes of God. When God blew into man's nostrils the breath of life and man became a living being (Gen. 2:7), the Spirit that came forth out of its own Essence, came to reside in mortal flesh to make it "live, move, and have its being" (Acts 17:28). In other words, the Spirit "localized" Itself by dwelling in man.

The ultimate purpose of Spirit life residing in man and woman is to make visible and tangible the manifold presence of the invisible God on the

Earth. Spirit life is not destined to remain permanently in mortal flesh but only to achieve the purpose for which it was sent. Once that mission has been completed or has served out its time on Earth, the Spirit residing in human beings then returns unto the Source from whence it came (Eccles. 12:7b). It is the moment of the "Great Release"!

In our daily living, we need to "get with the program" as to why we have been placed here on the Earth in the first place! It requires us to be sober and alert, realizing that we know neither the day nor the hour when the clock will stop ticking for each of us, signaling our time to exit STAGE LEFT and return to God as we were in the beginning.

The Word of God admonishes us, "But the day of the Lord will come like a thief, and then the heavens will pass away with a roar, and the heavenly bodies will be burned up and dissolved, and the earth and the works that are done on it will be exposed" (2 Pet. 3:10/ESV).

Surely, none of us as believers desires to be caught off guard when that moment arrives. Yet, the Scriptures remind us:

> But concerning that day or that hour, no one knows, not even the angels in heaven, nor the Son, but only the Father (Mark 13:32/ ESV).

> Watch therefore, for you know neither the day nor the hour (Matt. 25:13/ESV).

"Watching" consists of keeping in proper perspective that it is appointed unto us to die (Heb. 9:7). Our time here on Earth in the flesh is limited, like a flash in the pan, by the Zoom Effect. The Afterlife is for eternity. We should do all in our power to observe and do what God requires of us, namely, "only to do the right [thing] and to love goodness, and to walk humbly with [our] God" (Mic. 6:8/NAB) as we incarnate the Greatest Commandment, which is to love the Lord, our God, with all our heart and all our soul and all our mind and all our strength and to love our neighbor as ourselves (Matt. 28:30–31).

When that moment of the Great Release comes, we can only imagine anthropomorphically what will take place for each of us as we look upon our Elder Brother Jesus, who became our Lord and Savior, at the time of his glorified appearance in the heavenly realm. The lyrics of a popular song by Sandi Patty ignites the metaphor:

The sky shall unfold
Preparing His entrance
The stars shall applaud Him
With thunders of praise
The sweet light in His eyes
Shall enhance those awaiting
And we shall behold Him,
Then face to face.
And the angels shall sound
The shout of His coming
And the sleeping shall rise
From their slumbering place
And those who remain
Shall be changed in a moment
And we shall behold him
Then face to face.

When the spirit of the invisible God dwelling within each of us is released from its mortal confines and returns to the Source or Spirit from whence it came, we shall be as God is and live eternally IN God. There will be no more "weeping and wailing," for we shall be back HOME to live with and IN God for eternity!

So get ready for the Great Release!

CHAPTER 21

The Great Return

No one knows with absolute certainty or exactitude what occurs in that split, seismic moment when a person transitions from physical death to eternal life. It is known to the Creator alone. It is the greatest mystery of life yet to be unraveled. However, there are certain things that we can detect from the Scriptures as to what most likely will occur at that moment.

The psalmist, described as King David, boldly declared, "For thou wilt not leave my soul in hell; neither wilt thou suffer thine Holy One to see corruption. Thou wilt shew me the path of life: in thy presence is fulness of joy; at thy right hand there are pleasures for evermore" (Ps. 16:10–11/KJV).

The prophet Job cried out, "I know that my redeemer lives, and that in the end he will stand on the earth, And after my skin has been destroyed, yet in my flesh I will see God; I myself will see him with my own eyes — I, and not another. How my heart yearns within me" (Job 19:25–27/NIV).

Jesus, the Christ, said, "I am the resurrection and the life; whoever believes in me, even if he dies, will live, and everyone who lives and believes in me will never die. Do you believe this?" (John 11:25–26/NAB).

Jesus also declared, "Don't let your hearts be troubled. Trust in God, and trust also in me. There is more than enough room in my Father's home. If this were not so, would I have told you that I am going to prepare a place for you? When everything is ready, I will come and get you, so that you will always be with me where I am" (John 14:1–3/NLT).

The most-referenced biblical passage related to a life change after physical death is found in the apostle Paul's first letter to the nascent believers in Corinth:

> This I declare, brothers: flesh and blood cannot inherit the kingdom of God, nor does corruption inherit incorruption. Behold, I tell you a mystery. We shall not all fall asleep, but we will all be changed, in an instant, in the blink of an eye, at the last trumpet. For the trumpet will sound, the dead will be raised incorruptible, and we shall be changed. For that which is corruptible must clothe itself with incorruptibility, and that which is mortal must put on immortality. And when this which is corruptible clothes itself with incorruptibility and this which is mortal clothes itself with immortality, then the word that is written shall come about: "Death is swallowed up in victory; Where, O death, is your victory? Where, O death, is your sting?" (1 Cor. 15:50–55/NAB).

All of the above biblical passages present challenges in their apologetic descriptive narratives of the Afterlife, but all are certain about one core belief: There is life after physical death.

While we speak of life after death as the great "unknown," namely, not knowing its particulars, the Word of God is our reassurance that there is a continuation of life after death that defies human understanding and comprehension.

Against a backdrop of what has been ingrained in our mind and heart about the Afterlife, it is difficult to fathom that everyone we loved and everything we cherished in this life will be viewed as inconsequential and nonessential when the "Great Return" occurs. If you find it difficult to imagine everyone who has been created in the divine image and likeness of God returning to the Source and becoming one with It, then how do you explain how all the zillions of us, born on the Earth, came from within the same Source? Ours is not to figure out how; ours is to let God complete what He began in each of us from the moment we came forth from Him and were breathed into our mother's womb and became living beings.

All the concerns associated with the fleshly, material, or earthly life have no priority or place in God's dwelling. In eternal life, we will not be preoccupied with hunting down our loved ones who have preceded us in death. We will enter into God's presence as separate, individualized spiritual entities and be reunited in oneness with them within the totality of God's Essence. The family reunion will not consist of a gathering of hundreds or thousands, but will be celebrated in the context of all of us being subsumed and embedded in the oneness of God. We and God shall be one!

If married, the focus after death will not be on trying to find one's mate and being reconnected in matrimonial bliss for eternity. Married more than once? A person will not have to go through the discerning, excruciating process of deciding which spouse gets the eternal trophy.

Jesus, the Christ, quoted in the Gospel of Matthew, weighed in on the subject:

> They [Sadducees] put this question to him [Jesus], saying, "Teacher, Moses said, If a man dies without children, his brother shall marry his wife and raise up descendants for his brother. Now, there were seven brothers among them. The first married and died and, having no descendants, left his wife to his brother. The same happened with the second and the third, through all seven. Finally,

the woman died. Now, at the resurrection, of the seven, whose wife will she be? For they all had been married to her?" Jesus said to them in reply, "You are misled because you do not know the scriptures or the power of God. At the resurrection, they neither marry nor are given in marriage but are like the angels in heaven" (Matt. 22:23–30/NAB).

In the Afterlife, there will be no preoccupation with trying to catch up with what has happened to our loved ones since we last saw them. Even more so, there will not be countless individual spirits floating around who have preceded us in death, standing on the banks of the river anxiously awaiting souls to embrace and welcome to their eternal home.

We can still hold steadfastly to a belief in the ancestors, but from the vantage point of viewing all as one in God, not as separate entities gathering in assembly for a pep rally. In returning unto the Creator, all become absorbed in the Source and possess no separate identity apart from the One in whom all things ebb and flow.

There are a few biblical citations of characters appearing upon the Earth after physically dying, such as the spirit of Samuel being conjured up at En-dor, as well as Moses and Elijah appearing in the presence of the glorified Jesus on the Mount of Transfiguration. In these examples, the spirit of the deceased is present, not their physical form that allowed them to express their unique individuality while on Earth. Their earthly appearance in spirit is a reminder of their continued role in God's Providence, not an occasion for them to distinguish or separate themselves in activity from the Essence of God. Individuality is no more required of them to impact human endeavors than the spirit needing a body to distinguish it from another as an act of its own rather than of God.

Such a radical pronouncement flies in the face of what most of us have been taught about seeing and being with our loved ones again in the Afterlife and living with them happily ever after in eternal bliss. In the profound words of Saint John Chrysostom: "Those whom we have loved and lost are no longer where they were. They are now wherever we are." We, on Earth, can still commune with them while they dwell in another state of existence and experience their presence in our midst as we experience God's presence.

Communication brings about communion. The Church Triumphant (spiritual realm), namely, those who have overcome and conquered the forces of evil "by the blood of the Lamb and by the word of their testimony" (Rev. 12:11), stands united with the Church Militant (earthly realm), namely, those who are engaged in a struggle "with the principalities, with the powers, with the world rulers of this present darkness, with the evil spirits in the heavens" (Eph. 6:12). Heaven and Earth are one. Those bonds are strengthened when we, on Earth, are actively engaged and connected to those who have preceded us in death.

Such bold declarations can be too much for most people to handle who have been fed spiritual pablum all of their adult lives. The above-mentioned viewpoints are by no means an attempt to deny the existence of ancestors or persons who have intersected our lives while on Earth. In the words of twentieth-century writer François Mauriac in his work entitled *The Desert of Love*:

"We are, all of us, molded and re-molded by those who have loved us and even though that love may pass, we remain nonetheless their work — a work that very likely they do not recognize, which is never exactly what they intended. No love, no friendship can cross the path of our destiny without leaving some mark on it forever."

For the believer, God is real — God exists, even if God, in and of Himself, cannot be seen as a fleshly Being. The Scriptures state that no one can look upon God and continue living in the flesh (Exod. 33:20).

But how is it that we can communicate with an Entity that we have never seen? We commune and communicate with those who have died and spiritually ascended in exactly the same manner as we do with God. God is Spirit. They, too, are now one with God in Spirit.

Not only that, we believe that this Supreme Being hears and answers us through the medium of prayer. Prayer is the universal language that connects us to God and allows us to communicate with Him and those who have returned unto Him. The identity of the latter is one and the same as that of God, a seamless spiritual garment that cannot be tattered or torn asunder.

If you have believed in God all your life and in the power of God residing within you, then why would you not also believe that those who have returned unto God are now "like or as" God is (1 John 3:2) and possess the same essence and nature of the Godhead? In eternity, they are not known by their biologically given name as inscribed on their birth certificate. In dying, they shed their human name and reassume the fullness of their divine name before the foundations of the world were even laid. Their name, once again, as it was in the beginning before they were conceived in their mother's womb, is God.

When the moment of physical death occurs for each of us, we will know as God knows, and our concerns will be only those that pertain to God. Any worldly concern will have run its course, died, and gone to the grave. Our total focus will be from God's vantage point and God's perspective. We do not die to take upon ourselves earthly cares. We die to be freed from any and all things related to the demands of human life. The life that we will inherit is eternal. Nothing on Earth can stand in its path. The Negro spiritual, "Soon I Will Be Done" with the troubles of this world and go "home" to my Lord and be free, reminds us that we can take nothing with us from Earth to eternity.

God is Spirit, and only that which is of the Spirit can return unto God and become one with God. The apostle Paul admonished the early believers of "The Way" that "flesh and blood cannot inherit the kingdom of God, nor does corruption inherit incorruption" (1 Cor. 15:50/NAB).

Yes, the Word of God states emphatically that the Spirit of God dwelling within each of us will return unto the Source from whence it came (Eccles. 12:7b). We shall become one with the Divine Entity that breathed us forth from its own Essence.

The real identity we seek in the Afterlife is to dwell in God so we can take on the original identity that we possessed when God said, "Let us make man in our own image and likeness" (Gen. 1:26). The Great Return is about each of us taking on the fullness of God's Identity and consciousness as "it was in the beginning and ever shall be" so as to know only as God knows. In that manner, all that pertains to God and is within God's purview will be ours as well. There will be no need to hold on to any personal or individual identity or state of consciousness. It is released in the act of death so that God will be All in All.

Let us let God be God and allow Him to do what He does best. Let us leave the details of the Afterlife to God and trust that, in the moment of that great cataclysmic change, everything will be all right!

The Great Return awaits each and every one of us! So, get ready for the greatest experience of a lifetime!

CHAPTER 22

Oneness Is about Inclusion, Not Individuality

G od the Creator of all things is one. The creation of the world by God proceeded out of oneness and has always been about achieving oneness. Genesis 1:1 states, "In the beginning, when God created ..." Everything ebbs and flows out of it.

All human life originates out of the oneness of God and will ultimately return to become one with the Source from whence it came. Each individual created in the image and likeness of God bears the divine traits, characteristics, and attributes of the Creator. One of those qualities is uniqueness. The very fact that no two individuals are exactly alike reflects the multiplicity of God's Essence. It is through a person's individuality that they uniquely manifest the nature of the invisible God on Earth.

What is the true meaning and purpose of individuality? Individuality is defined as "the particular character, or aggregate of qualities, that distinguishes one person or thing from others" (Dictionary.com). A person uses their uniqueness to achieve in the flesh their particular vocation or calling in life.

Once an individual's earthly assignment has purposed itself, the spirit or breath that made the person "live, move, and have their being" (Acts

17:28/NAB) returns to become one with the Source, as it was in the beginning, when the idea of their existence in the mind of God became reality in the flesh.

While it might seem somewhat disconcerting or unfathomable that a person "releases" their individuality back to God at the time of physical death, the point is that their individuality came out of the identity of God. The life that we possess belongs to God. As the apostle Paul writes, "None of us lives for oneself, and no one dies for oneself. For if we live, we live for the Lord, and if we die, we die for the Lord; so then, whether we live or die, we are the Lord's" (Rom. 14:7–8/NAB).

We never owned individuality from the beginning. Even though God bestows it upon us at the moment of conception, it does not belong to us forever. Individuality is not an eternal keepsake. It must be subsumed back into the oneness of the individuality of God. It is given or bestowed upon us for a "season." Individuality has no place in the Kingdom of Heaven. It serves no useful purpose. In fact, in human life, we are partakers in God's divinity, identity, and individuality. All and everything that is of us must surrender itself to God, our Heavenly Parent and Creator, and become completely and totally absorbed in Him. As Paul stated, "I have been crucified with Christ and I no longer live, but Christ lives in me. The life I now live in the body, I live by faith in the Son of God, who loved me and gave himself for me" (Gal. 2:20/NIV).

In his Priestly Prayer, Jesus pleaded for *oneness* in uttering these words to God, his Father and Heavenly Parent: "I pray not only for them, but also for those who will believe in me through their word, so that they may all be one, as you, Father, are in me and I in you, that they also may be in us, that the world may believe that you have sent me" (John 17:20–21/NAB).

The Gospel of John is quite clear about divine union being the ultimate goal of the spiritual life. It is still the central message and promise of the Gospel. Oneness is the goal, not just in heart and mind but in spirit as well. What Jesus envisioned was a mutual indwelling, namely, "I am in God, God is in you, you are in God, and we are in each other; therefore, we are one." Both the one and the many are held together in the One, the eternal Godhead.

Jesus's entire earthly mission was based and centered on becoming one with God, not only in this life but in the life to come, at the time of the Great Return and calling his followers to do the same. He was of oneness in mind, heart, spirit, and purpose. Jesus achieved this through the uniqueness of his individuality. The fullness and totality of the invisible Essence of God was so powerfully rooted and manifested in his earthly life that he and God became one. Jesus said, "Whoever sees me, sees my Father." Thus, as a unique individual called and chosen by God, he became for humankind "the Way, the Truth, and the Life" (John 14:6/KJV).

The key that opens the door to an understanding about individuality, oneness, and inclusion is Jesus. He, being the "firstborn" in "the image of the invisible God" (Col. 1:15/NAB), came out of Oneness. The premise is based upon Jesus not having been born upon the Earth as fully God. Through a process of becoming the "Source" of eternal salvation by obedience to the Word of God and by the things he suffered (Heb. 5:8), Jesus became fully God and fully man. His entire public ministry centered on the Kingdom of God and its call to righteousness and repentance. Man and woman had lost their way and needed a messiah to restore them to their original state as sinless children of God. A satanic pandemic had invaded the planet, creating hybrid beings possessing both good and evil. Humankind was in need of healing and restoration.

For the historical Jesus, it was never a "me thing." It was about becoming completely absorbed in the intentionality of the will of his Father and accomplishing it. His earthly mission was to restore the Kingdom of God on Earth. The Scriptures clearly state that Jesus came into this life to do the will of his Father, and not his own will: "Amen, amen. I say to you, a son cannot do anything on his own, but only what he sees his father doing; for what he does, his son will do also" (John 5:19/NAB). Jesus was here in this world to serve God and humanity.

Again, it is stated in verse 30 that "I cannot do anything on my own … because I do not seek my own will but the will of the one who sent me." Although he was an absolutely unique individual, Jesus never sought personal acclaim or recognition of his words or deeds. His real identity never allowed him to forget why he was sent, and it undergirded him as a righteous individual.

Individuality served its purpose in Jesus's life and was not diminished by his return to the Father. And the same will apply to each of us if we follow in the footsteps of Jesus.

Life has never been solely about us — or, at least, it should not be! Rather, it is about each of us using the unique giftedness and talents of our individuality in bringing all things into conformity with the oneness that all of us possess in God, our Heavenly Parent and Creator of all things. In the words of Rev. Jim Baker, "[We] are already one with everything. All that is absent is our awareness. Through awareness it becomes apparent that separateness of the one from the many is an illusion. Slowly we begin to see that both the one and the many are held together in the One, the Eternal Godhead. And as we come to know our self within this One, we also come to know our oneness with all that is held by the One. Awareness allows us to know this reality, and our cooperation with the Spirit allows this awareness to become transformational" ("What Does the Bible Say about Oneness?"/SacredStructures.org).

In the final analysis, it is not about having a perpetual hold on our individuality once it has served its primary and essential purpose in manifesting the "glory of God fully alive in man [and] the life of man being the vision of God" (Irenaeus, an Early Church Father). Individuality serves as a handmaid in achieving the purpose in life for which we were sent forth. Individuality, as typically understood on the earthly plane, has no place in the Spirit World, commonly known as Heaven. It is all about oneness, unity, and inclusion.

However, "be not dismayed whatever betide." A person's individuality will not die. It will last on the Earth in memoriam on many different levels. History will serve as the preserver of a person's uniqueness and individuality in its accounts of the impact and contributions each individual has made on the human landscape. Ancestor worship or veneration in many countries of the world serves as a reminder that our loved ones have not died eternally but continue to intervene on many different levels in the personal lives of those left behind. Religion, particularly Roman Catholicism and Orthodoxy, pays tribute to individuals by declaring them as saints for public and private devotion and emulation. Their earthly lives are offered as shining examples of how to live in a holy and righteous manner. Individuality has its place on Earth and should always be celebrated. However, in the realm of the Spirit, there will be no shrines or monuments dedicated or erected to individualism. Everything will be as one within the Source, and all focus will be directed on Him.

If a person's individuality is to serve the purpose in life for which God created him or her, then what is the use of individuality once it has fulfilled its mission and there is no longer life present in the body? What purpose will my individuality serve in the Afterlife? What value does my individuality have in Heaven?

There will be "no seating at the right hand" or any sitting at banquet tables in Heaven because sitting is a biological or human function, not a spiritual activity. Heaven is a state of spiritual habitation. The Sacred Writers employed the technique of anthropomorphic language in describing spiritual concepts in human constructs so their listeners could envision or get a grasp on them. Unfortunately, it contributed to believers embracing the idea of Heaven as a place in the sky in the "sweet by and by" with all of the accoutrements of Earth in endless supply. The hymn "Dwelling in Beulah Land" by C. Austin Miles is a classic example:

> I'm living on the mountain, underneath a cloudless sky,
> I'm drinking at the fountain that never shall run dry;
> Oh, yes! I'm feasting on the manna from a bountiful supply,
> For I am dwelling in Beulah Land.

God created us as His children (made "in our image"), which is why He's called *Father* or, in Jesus's words, *Daddy* (*Abba*), and therefore we will always be children of God. But once His children have returned unto Him, they become one with and in Him, as He is: "Beloved, we are God's children now; what we shall be has not yet been revealed. We do know that when it is revealed we shall be like Him, for we shall see Him as He is" (1 John 3:2/NAB).

After I am dead, my individuality vanishes "like an evening gone, short as the watch that ends the night before the rising sun" ("O God, Our Help in Ages Past," v. 4). It does not belong to me, and I can take no ultimate credit for whatever may be achieved or accomplished in the process of utilizing it. It must be returned eventually to the One who gave it. Returning my individuality to the Creator in no way, shape, or form minimizes its uniqueness or contribution to humanity. It only affirms and validates it.

Once my physical life is done, my purpose in life is finished and I yield it back to the Source from whence it came. Did not Jesus say from the Cross after he had received the sour wine, "'It is finished,' and he bowed his head and gave up his spirit" (John 19:30)? Nothing else mattered at that point. All praise, glory, and honor belonged to the One who initiated the divine life within and received it back unto Himself. A person's individuality no longer serves any purpose in the Afterlife. When all is said and done, individuality must give way to inclusion so that all may be one.

Yet, there is another school of thought that holds steadfastly to the belief that individuality remains intact after a person's death and the spirit within returns to the Source from whence it came. This objection has a biblical foundation (Gen. 1:27, 1 John 3:1–2, and others). So, from this perspective, the purpose of individuality in the Afterlife is to provide God, the Heavenly Parent, with children whom He can continue to love for eternity and who can love Him and give Him joy for eternity!

To this author, the basis for his firm belief is also embedded in the Scriptures. All life originated from the same Source and came out of oneness. It is into that Source of oneness that we shall all return and become one with It. Although each person was an idea in the mind of God before the divine breath was blown into mortal flesh and came forth in reality as an individual (each person possessing a particular aspect of God's individuality), we ultimately surrender that individuality back to the Source and become as God is (1 John 3:2). Our unique and personal individuality will not be annihilated once we physically die, but it will serve no useful purpose in the Spirit World apart from its identity with the individuality of God. God's individuality then will become our individuality because everything originates and ends in Him. We are all subsumed into the Essence of God.

The perennial challenge for the believer is spiritually maturing as a person who achieves, establishes, and maintains the oneness out of which he or she came until they ultimately return to the Source and become one with It in all things.

Unfortunately, conventional, conservative theology and catechesis do not aid in the process of truly developing a spiritual mindset that sees creation, people, and all things as one. Listen to the sagacious words of a well-versed Christian pastor, Jim Baker:

> [As Christians,] we use biblical terms like Christlikeness, having a personal relationship with Jesus, and being Christ's disciples to convey the call to be Christians, or "little Christs." Yet, oneness is also a biblical term and in many respects conveys a different, if not deeper meaning. My Evangelical language refers to God more as a Father and Jesus more as a friend than as Spirit that lives and moves within me. Again, both are true. The difference though is that one portrays a more outside in relationship, while the other an inside out relationship. One portrays a split with God while the other conveys a union with God. One refers to a concrete relationship and the other an abstract expression of the divine mystery of the God-given Godly nature of ourselves. And, one sees us as having to find God, the other that God is already here, all about us, and within us — the very source and fulfillment of our being. That is why the mystical expressions of faith focus so much on meditation and contemplation: that we might awaken to God's presence all about us and within us.
>
> Biblical oneness speaks also to our oneness with each other and all of creation. This type of oneness was taught in the earliest expressions of Christianity but was regretfully lost along the

way. The "separate than" language that emerged over the centuries created a dualistic mindset and has created the optical illusion of separateness. We set boundaries to establish individuality but what we get is isolation and alienation. We distinguish ourselves from nature and we end up exploiting the environment. We think of ourselves as separate from people who aren't like us, and the result is racism and prejudice. Eventually, our dualism causes us to no longer distinguish that we are intimately interrelated with God and all creation, and deny ourselves unfettered participation in life with God, others, and the natural world ("What Is Oneness with God?"/SacredStructures.org).

When the above-quoted pastor talks about oneness with God, oneness with Jesus, oneness with other people, and oneness with all things, he has in mind a oneness in heart in which individuality is retained on each side. His thesis is that, just as when we "merge" in oneness with other people or with "all things" in the environment, it's an empathy of the heart — the same mystical empathy of the heart that occurs when we're born again in a relationship with Jesus or when we're caught up in the bliss of a relationship with God, as was the case with Saint Teresa of Ávila or Saint John of the Cross.

Saint Augustine of Hippo (354–430), one of the greatest Church Fathers of the early Christian church, stated in his magnum opus, *Confessions*, "You have made us for Yourself, and our hearts are restless until they can find rest in You."

What is sought on the mystical level is at the core of achieving it on the spiritual level, where the spirit of God present in us unites and becomes one with the Spirit of God. Paul alluded to this when he wrote to the Roman church, "The Spirit itself bears witness with our spirit that we are children of God, and if children, then heirs, heirs of God and joint heirs with Christ" (Rom. 8:16–17/NAB). Once we become full heirs of the promises of God, the spirit of God dwelling within each of us becomes one as God is.

A loss of oneness in our world has made it difficult to realize and actualize a spiritual way of thinking that leads back to a profound understanding that it is not about "you or me" but about "all of us" becoming as it was in the beginning — oneness in spirit, not oneness in flesh. The apostle Paul urged his hearers, "Do not conform yourself to this age but be transformed by the renewal of your mind, that you may discern what is the will of God, what is good and pleasing and perfect" (Rom. 12:2/NAB).

What is the will of God? It is contained in the Priestly Prayer of Jesus that still cries out for fulfillment, "that they may all be one" (John 17:21/NAB).

Reflect upon these biblical passages that echo becoming one with and in God:

> But whoever is joined to the Lord becomes one spirit with Him (1 Cor. 6:17/NAB).

> But we all, with unveiled faces, looking as in a mirror at the glory of the Lord, are being transformed into the same image from glory to glory, just as from the Lord, the Spirit (2 Cor. 3:18/NASB).

> But whoever keeps His Word, truly the love of God is perfected in him. By this we know that we are in Him (1 John 2:5/NKJV).

He [Jesus] was in the beginning with God (John 1:2/NAB).

I and My Father are one (John 10:30/NKJV).

[Concerning the fact that we were created as "gods":] Jesus answered them, "Is it not written in your law, 'I said, "You are gods [Ps. 8:6]"'? If it calls them gods to whom the word of God came, and scripture cannot be set aside, can you say that the one whom the Father has consecrated and sent into the world blasphemes because I said, 'I am the Son of God'?" (John 10:34-36/NAB).

Our goal both in physical and eternal life is not to become a shrine to polytheism but to manifest the "wonders" of our monotheistic God. Once that mission has been completed, we return back to "home base" and surrender all, including our individuality, to God. It is in that moment that we become one with God and God is all in all (1 Cor. 15:18).

When all is said and done, it will be about inclusion in oneness, not individuality in multiplicity.

CHAPTER 23

Welcome Home!

When you think of Heaven, what images race across your mind or flood your soul? Do you think of Heaven as "Home"? There is an expression that says, "Home is where the heart is." I believe that the true Heaven we are seeking resides in the Heart of God. When a person spiritually grows up, there is no need to have an attachment to anything material or physical to achieve happiness and fulfillment. As spirit beings returning to the fullness of God when our earthen nature ceases, a material structure is not needed.

The fourteenth chapter of the Gospel of John speaks of Jesus, the Christ, telling his disciples:

> Let not your heart be troubled: ye believe in God, believe also in me. In my Father's house there are many mansions: if it were not so, I would have told you. I go to prepare a place for you. And if I go and prepare a place for you, I will come again, and receive you unto myself; that where I am, there ye may be also (John 14:1–3/KJV).

Many believers have been mistakenly misled by this passage, as if Jesus were saying to his followers that they could anticipate inheriting a material mansion upon entry into the Kingdom of Heaven. Where would that so-called mansion be located? On Grace Boulevard and Mercy Street?

Nothing could be further from the truth! That which is material (corruptible) cannot exist in a state of incorruptibility (1 Cor. 15:50). *Mansion* is a symbolic expression referring to the many spiritual "levels or degrees" in God's presence rather than to the bestowal of a physical property upon death. If a person, as spirit, inherited a "mansion," it would limit or constrict that person to a particular time and space. It would be antithetical to the ubiquitous and unbridled nature of spirit, which is anywhere and everywhere at the same time.

What would the material properties of Jesus's statement "In my Father's house there are many mansions" consist of? Think about it. Just how many zillions of "mansions" can a so-called place like Heaven hold? Where would all the "mansions" be located if there is a "mansion" reserved for every person who ever died? It really doesn't make any sense at all.

First of all, Jesus says, "Let not your heart be troubled." The clue to unlocking the meaning of the passage is contained in the word *heart*. Why did Jesus reference the "heart"? Because the only way for the "heart" not to be troubled is for it to rest itself in the "Heart of God." Saint Augustine of Hippo said, "Our hearts are restless until they rest in Thee."

Death does not release the heart (soul and spirit) from the confines of an earthly physical structure only for it to inherit another entanglement or material housing. The beauty of death is that it frees us from anything and everything that constricts or limits our movements. We become as God is.

The "place" where Jesus said he would go and prepare a place for us is related to each of us dwelling in the fullness of the Essence of God where he also resides. Jesus and the Father are one. In what many biblical scholars call the *Priestly Prayer*, Jesus prayed these words to his Father and our Father:

I pray not only for them, but also for those who will believe in me through their word, so that they may all be one, as you, Father, are in me and I in you, that they also may be in us, that the world may believe that you sent me. And I have given them the glory you gave me, so that they may be one, as we are one. I in them and you in me, that they may be brought to perfection as one, that the world may know that you sent me, and that you loved them even as you loved me. Father, they are your gift to me. I wish that where I am they also may be with me, that they may see my glory that you gave me, because you loved me before the foundation of the world. Righteous Father, the world also does not know you, but I know you and they know that you sent me. I made known to them your name and I will make it known, that the love with which you loved me may be in them and I in them (John 17:20–26/NAB).

Spiritual perfection is achieved when the spirit of God that resides within our mortal frame returns to the Source from whence it came and becomes one with God as it was in the beginning prior to being breathed into corruptible flesh. Heaven is about becoming one with God. It is not about the acquisition of a mansion in the sky, supping at an endless banqueting feast, or being bedecked with precious jewels while wearing a crown and clad in long white robes with feet shod in golden Nike slippers!

Dorothy, the protagonist in the movie *The Wiz*, sang in the hit song "Home,"

When I think of home, I think of a place
Where there's love overflowing
I wish I were home, I wish I was back there
With the things I've been knowin'

What you and I have been "knowin'" is not what "home" or "mansion" symbolizes when it comes to the things of God. Our minds seem incapable of grasping that which is beyond our understanding. They are calibrated to comprehend only the material, not the ethereal.

If God, as Spirit, does not need a "house" to dwell in, then why should we expect to live in a "mansion" at the point when the flesh can afford us a home no longer? In the Old Testament (as quoted in the Book of Acts), the Word of God states,

> "But Solomon built a house for [God]. Yet the Most High does not dwell in houses made by human hands. As the prophet says: 'The heavens are my throne, the earth is my footstool. What kind of house can you build for me? says the Lord, or what is to be my resting place? Did not my hand make all these things?'" (Acts 7:47–50/NAB).

In the New Testament, Jesus states, "And if I go and prepare a place for you, I will come again, and receive you unto myself; that where I am, there ye may be also" (John 14:3/NAB). Jesus comes to take us with him so that we can be with him where he resides. To receive a person unto oneself is for the two to become one, just as Adam received Eve unto himself and the two became one flesh (Gen. 2:24). In death, we become one in the Spirit, as Jesus is one with God, our Heavenly Parent, and we are one in Him.

Home is the place where the love of God abounds. Love, after physical death, does not reside in a material or physical structure. It resides in the Heart of God. And, that Heart is where Heaven dwells and where we will be one with God in all things.

Welcome Home!

How God Resolves Loneliness

In the beginning, only God existed.

The opening verses of Genesis state, "In the beginning, when God created the heavens and the earth, the earth was a formless wasteland, and darkness covered the abyss, while a mighty wind swept over the waters" (Gen. 1:1–2/NAB).

Everything that came to be was a resultant activity of the creative powers or energy of a Divine Being. Believers address this Entity by a variety of names. The predominant religion uses the term "God." The Scriptures state that "God is Spirit, and those who worship him must worship in Spirit and truth" (John 4:24/NAB).

The totality of God's Essence or nature is Spirit. Since God is the only One who existed prior to the beginning, residing IN AND OF HIMSELF, there was no one present in the entire universe for God to love until God created someone in His image and likeness to be the recipient of that love. Love cannot be spoken of in abstraction — nor can it be realized in and of itself. It needs a love object to manifest itself. According to the Book of Genesis,

The Lord God said: "It is not good for man to be alone. I will make a suitable partner for him." So the Lord God formed out of the ground various wild animals and various birds of the air, and he brought them to the man to see what he would call them; whatever the man called each of them would be its name. The man gave names to all the cattle, all the birds of the air, and all the wild animals; but none proved to be the suitable partner for the man. So the Lord God cast a deep sleep on the man, and while he was asleep, he took out one of his ribs and closed up its place with flesh. The Lord God then built up into a woman the rib that he had taken from the man. When he brought her to the man, the man said: "This one, at last, is bone of my bones and flesh of my flesh; This one shall be called woman, for out of her man this one has been taken" (Gen. 2:18–23/NAB).

Just as Adam did not find a suitable partner after God had provided for all his material needs, one can imagine that neither did God find a suitable partner to impart the fullness of His Love after having creating the entire universe. It was no mere coincidence that God saved the best for last by creating us. So, God said, "Let us make man in our image, after our likeness" (Gen. 1:26/NAB). No one or nothing could return a satisfying or comparable love back to God unless that entity bore a resemblance to the Godhead.

God cannot be spoken of as Love (1 John 4:16) unless there is "give-and-take action." It was for that very reason that God formed and fashioned man and woman to resemble God and thus be capable of achieving a level of spiritual perfection where they could reach the summit of the Godself. Jesus said to his disciples, "Be perfect, therefore, as your heavenly Father is perfect" (Matt. 5:48/NIV).

As individuals, we express a love for God on the vertical level. Love is made visible and tangible by the way we love one another on the horizontal level. It is summarized in the Greatest Commandment, uttered by Jesus: "Love the Lord your God with all your heart and with all your soul and with all your mind. This is the first and greatest commandment. And the second is like it: 'Love your neighbor as yourself.' All the Law and the Prophets hang on these two commandments" (Matt. 22:37–40/NIV).

God made us primarily to receive His love. In creating us, God could have said, "I am the Lovemaker. I give the world love." In turn, it is that same love of God that calls us to be lovemakers as we give love to one another on the human plane. As God's love partners, fidelity requires us to return love back to God in a visible and tangible way by demonstrating how we love one another. Love is brought to perfection when we see God within ourselves and strive to discover that same presence in others. In that way, love becomes real and genuine (1 John 4:17).

But what happens when a person we love, especially someone who is significant or means the world to us, is no longer visibly present among us? Do we lose it, fall apart, and disintegrate? Does it seem that the God in whom we trusted all our lives has abandoned or forsaken us? Do we think, how could God leave us in such a miserable and unpredictable state of mind? Does God really care about us being left behind with only sorrow, troubles, and loneliness as our life's companions? Where is God in this picture?

Did it ever cross your mind that God came up with a formula for resolving loneliness a long, long time ago? While there is no direct scriptural passage that states that God experienced loneliness or a state of being lonely, there are ample verses in the Bible that clearly show that God has an emotional side. For instance, God regretted ever having created man (Gen.

6:6), and there are a plethora of examples of God's wrath and anger displayed as a result of His displeasure with people's acts of disobedience. Just to cite a few biblical references: Deuteronomy 9:9, Exodus 15:7, Numbers 11:1–2, Job 4:9, and 2 Kings 13:3. Therefore, a state of loneliness is not outside the parameters of God's nature.

Man and woman were formed and fashioned in God's image and likeness not solely for the purpose of being the earthen vessels to hold the Spirit of God (2 Cor. 4:7). They were also made to activate the spirit within through worship. True worship consists of more than paying homage or reverence to the invisible God. It involves a complete surrender to God's will and a total commitment to manifesting God's love for all humanity. In this way is love made divine when it presents itself as a visible and tangible expression of the God within:

"We have come to know and to believe in the love God has for us. God is love, and whoever remains in love remains in God and God in him. In this is love brought to perfection among us, that we have confidence on the day of judgment because as he is, so are we in this world" (1 John 4:16–17/NAB).

As long as there is a God, man and woman can triumph over loneliness because perfect love always needs a recipient or love object. There is always "a ram in the bush"! Even when the spirit of the Living God residing within each and every one of us returns to the Source from whence it came, God will not only love us eternally in the Afterlife but will continue to bring forth spiritual life clothed in flesh upon the Earth that will fill the void. Why? Because God is love and love is eternal. Therefore, God will not be lonely, nor will we, because God has made ample provision for man and woman to be the eternal love partners of God, which dissolves the pangs of loneliness.

If you want to avoid the permanent sting of loneliness, then love as God has loved us. The God we love is always there in Spirit, and so are those who have returned unto God. Let us commune with them as we do with God. Eternity awaits us to experience the power of love that knows no end and banishes every form of loneliness when we all eventually become as God is.

Now you know how God resolves loneliness.

CHAPTER 24

Prayer: The Great Communicator

We can communicate with those who have physically died and now live in the Spirit World in the same way and manner that we commune with a God whom we have never seen. When the spirit expires and leaves the body, it returns to the same Source from whence it came (Eccles. 12:7). The apostle Paul reminds us in his second letter to the Christian church at Corinth that "to be absent from the body is to be present with the Lord" (2 Cor. 5:8). While many Christians have uttered this passage ad nauseam, they fail to realize and appreciate its fullest meaning and significance. If the spirit is no longer present in the body, then where is it? It has left the building (temple) to return to its original dwelling place, namely, back to be subsumed and embedded in the very Essence of God, who is Spirit. That which was of God in the beginning returns in the end to become one with God. The spirit or breath takes on the same identity, nature, purpose, and function of God.

As believers, we have been taught since childhood that the way to communicate with God is through prayer. While none of us has ever seen or touched God, we have come to believe that God not only exists but hears and answers prayers. Many of us never even questioned the concept but accepted and embraced it through faith — hook, line, and sinker!

Just imagine, not only talking to someone whom we have never seen but believing in the depths of our being that such an Entity will respond and answer us! If we can communicate with God, who is ever present in the Spirit World, so can we communicate in the same fashion with those who no longer reside in the flesh but live in the totality of the fullness of God.

We operate in the presence of the Spirit World each and every day without realizing it. The Spirit World is an ever-present reality and is never absent from us. In fact, Earth is encapsulated in it! The Kingdom of God is in our midst (Luke 17:21), and most of the time we are not even aware of it!

Why would we not think that we can function in the same manner and feel the same connection with our loved ones who have passed on as we do in relating to God? It is probably because we were never taught in Sunday school classes or our Baltimore Catechism lessons about the correlation between the Divinity of God and how that divinity dwells within each of us. God was portrayed always as above and beyond our grasp, possessing a divine nature totally and distinctively different from our own. We were never told the primary reason for our existence on Earth, namely, to manifest in a visible and tangible way the glory and presence of the invisible God dwelling within us. The Early Church Father Irenaeus was right on point when he stated, "the glory of God is man [and woman] fully alive, but the life of man [and woman] is the vision of God."

Unfortunately, many believers can neither fathom nor embrace a way of life that ultimately leads to becoming as God is. Instead, most opt for pursuing a path that, in their minds, will lead to achieving Heaven by living a holy life in an "I/Thou" relationship with God on a vertical plane. It is a relationship that barely connects on the horizontal plane by envisioning those who have died as possessing the same nature as God. Therein lies the crux of the problem: a failure to understand the relationship that exists between those who remain physically upon the Earth and those who have returned to the fullness of God in the Spirit World.

The power of prayer manifests when it connects the spiritual world with the terrestrial. It lets those who are left behind to be spiritually present with those "who have gone before us marked with the sign of faith" and are now asleep in God. The Gospel of John 4:24 states, "God is Spirit, and those who worship him must worship in Spirit and truth" (NAB). The way we relate in worship to God and stay connected to our loved ones who have preceded us in death is through the medium of prayer. It is a form of spiritual channeling that allows us to never forget that, "in death, life is changed, not ended."

CHAPTER 25

How to Communicate with Loved Ones in the Spirit World

Before there was an "In the beginning" (Gen. 1:1) there was only the Spirit World! The Progenitor of all things, whom we call God, the Creator, IS! In God, there is no past or future, only the existential and eternal moment that is called the "IS or PRESENT"! All of creation is linked to this Source and takes its beginning, end, meaning, purpose, and fulfillment in alignment with it.

Man and woman, as external forms, are a composition of dirt and water. As such, that which comprises the visible can be compared to a deflated balloon. When air is inserted into the rubber mass, it expands and reaches its intended function, which is to soar above the heights. In like manner, "air" is the invisible property that fills the body to give it life. Although it cannot be seen, its presence is required within the mass to sustain it.

In theological terms, we speak of this air as *ruah* (Hebrew), *pneuma* (Greek), and *wind* or *breath*. God breathed (spiritual) into the nostrils (corporeal) of man and woman, and they became living beings/souls (Gen. 2:7). That which makes them in God's image and likeness is, therefore, Spirit, not flesh! The Spirit of the Living God is housed in an earthen vessel of clay to show that the excellency of God's creation belongs to the Creator and not to ourselves: "But we have this treasure in earthen vessels, so that the surpassing greatness of the power will be of God and not from ourselves" (2 Cor. 4:7/NAB).

As essentially spirit beings robed or clothed in flesh, man and woman have the capacity to commune with the Spirit World through the power of the Spirit present within them. The Spirit of God in them is identical with the Source from whence they received life. There is no life apart from the Spirit. If God, as Spirit, has Intelligence that can commune with mortal flesh, then the Spirit of God residing in flesh can ascend to a level where it can interact and correspond with its Creator as well as with the deceased who have returned unto God. Spirit must speak to Spirit in a language that is universal!

In most faith circles, that universal language is called *prayer*. Whenever we pray to God, we are speaking to the One who is the Owner of the Spirit World. But not only that, we are communing with those who have returned to the fullness of God's Essence and are now embedded within the very nature of God. This profound spiritual principle is highlighted in the twelfth chapter of the Book of Ecclesiastes, verse 7: "And the dust returns to the ground it came from, and the spirit returns to God who gave it" (NIV).

If we have communed for a lifetime with a God who is Spirit and whom we have never seen, then how is it that we cannot hold on to that same belief when it comes to communicating with the same Spirit of God that was housed in the recesses of a deceased loved one? We believe in a God whom we have never seen, yet fail to see God dwelling in a brother or sister whom we see every day (1 John 4:19–21).

Oftentimes, our belief system is not properly aligned with our "grief system." At the death of a loved one, we grieve uncontrollably at the loss, as if there were no longer any hope of communicating with them or of feeling their continued presence among us. We think that we must "let go" or say goodbye or farewell to them, as if they have been taken from us.

Some pastors and preachers even attempt to lessen the pain by comforting the bereaved with the soothing words "we loved him/her but God loved him/her best." What kind of illogical nonsense is that? You mean to tell me, pastor, that the depths of God's love is expressed by taking away (my mother, father, spouse, child) the one person whom I loved and cherished? No wonder so many people have stopped believing in God with such pronouncements of foolery!

Even more misconstrued is the mixed message conveyed to those left behind whose loved one has died! God saw just how much they were suffering so He decided to gently close their eyes and give them eternal rest. How disconcerting! God does not cause anyone to die, not the young or old, just or unjust, good or bad, straight or gay, tall or short, fat or skinny, Black or White, rich or poor. God is the Author and Giver of life, not the Bestower of death! In fact, death is the one entity that makes no accommodation or discrimination. It strikes when and where it wills.

God only intervenes AFTER physical death has occurred. It is then and only then that God steps in and calls the spirit that resided within mortal flesh back home to its place of origination! To say that God calls us out of this life by bringing on death only for us to enter into eternal life is downright false! It would imply that God is a Killer and commits homicide and that He in some way has distanced Himself, and those who have died, from us. No, death makes our loved ones more present and active in our lives — indeed, more so than they were while alive in the flesh. It gives them the full operational powers of the Spirit Creator who is omnipotent, omniscient, and omnipresent.

If you believe that you can commune and communicate with God, who is a Pure Spirit Entity, then let your belief system ascend to embrace the same faith in regard to your expired loved ones who have become one with God in all things and in all ways! Talking and hearing from your loved ones who have physically died and spiritually ascended is not voodoo or hoodoo. It is what "you do" to remain one with them both in life and death. As the Word of God boldly proclaims, "Death is swallowed up in victory. O death, where is thy sting? O grave, where is thy victory?" (1 Cor. 15:57).

CHAPTER 26

A Word to Those Who Minister to the Bereaved

Peace be with you, my beloved and esteemed colleagues in ordained ministry. I extremely value our divine calling. I believe that each of us has been chosen providentially by God to be the spiritual bridge between Him and those whom He has appointed us to serve. For many of us, ministry is everything! It conveys to the believer the reason for which we were born and what we deem as our purpose and mission in life. When we celebrate the rituals of our respective faith traditions, we embody God's presence among humanity and become the transmitters of God's love, grace, mercy, divine favor, and compassion to God's people.

The most difficult challenge that any of us could ever encounter in ministry is ministering to those who have lost a cherished loved one. Nothing can replace a deceased parent, grandparent, grandchild, spouse, significant other, child, or sibling. Knowing how to approach the situation from a pastoral perspective that will bring comfort and consolation to the bereaved is no easy task. How do you fill the hole or vacuum, the emptiness created by such a loss? Words often seem so inadequate and frivolous in explaining human loss. When a loved one succumbs to the physical forces of death, those left behind often grieve inconsolably, collapse, and lose all sense of hope and direction. They seem incapable of making the necessary adjustments required to view physical death from a different perspective, seeing it as an ending that creates a chasm between themselves and their loved one. Death seems to slam a door right in their faces!

None of us is exempt from the reality of death. We all have experienced it personally within our own clerical ranks and families. Understanding that it is the most painful, gut-wrenching situation in the lives of those left behind, we are more than aware that our ministerial mettle will be put to the test. What do we say and how do we say it to ease the pain of the bereaved, both in reaching out to the family through grief counseling as well as delivering a message of hope in eternal life?

How do we convey to the individual or family what "thus saith the Lord" about the meaning of life and death? How do we administer a balm that can make the wounded whole? Do we continue to expound upon the myths of bygone years by trumpeting that their loved one has "flown away" to a place in the sky called Heaven where "walls of jasper, streets of purest gold, and twelve gates to the city await them"? How many times have we proclaimed that the deceased are in another place, high above us, looking down lovingly and tenderly upon us, and comforting us in our grief?

Last, how do we provide solace to those left behind, assuring them that their deceased loved one lives on in the fullness of a reality that we have yet to experience? Can they remain in communion with their loved one or must they go through the agonizing process of saying goodbye, farewell, or until we meet again? How do you, as a pastor or minister, convey a sense that their loved one has not left them for a journey to a distant place beyond the sky in the "sweet by and by," but remains with them in the form of a spirit, just as God, who is Spirit, dwells among them?

The book *Beyond the Zoom: The Afterlife* seeks to respond to the questions as to how we, as ministers of the Gospel, can impart the Word of God about the meaning of life and death that will assist in bringing about a paradigm shift in the way the faithful have viewed death all their lives. This paradigm shift can transport the grieving believer to a new understanding of physical death. Through connecting the biblical dots related to life and death, the words contained within the pages of this book will provide greater comfort and inner peace to those dealing with the loss of a loved one.

Words can be so inadequate in providing comfort to the bereaved, especially when they are ill prepared to hear them. Believe it or not, most of those experiencing loss do not want to hear about a loving, just, and merciful God in the initial stages of their grief or to be comforted when in the midst of denial. They are going through the various stages of grief and haven't even gotten anywhere close to resignation and acceptance (see *On Death and Dying*, by Elisabeth Kübler-Ross). At the moment of a loved one's death, in most instances all they want to do is cry their hearts out and perhaps withdraw and be left alone to wallow in their uncontrollable grief. It is not that they do not believe in the Afterlife or desire your presence. They simply need personal space to have their personal moment to express grief and work it out in their own way, in their own time, and under their own terms.

However, timing is everything. You have to possess a sense of timing as to when is the appropriate moment to reach out, the frequency of the contact, what to say, and, most importantly, what not to say when the opportunity conveniently presents itself to comfort the bereaved.

Whatever pastoral approach is taken to comfort and minister to the bereaved, I encourage you with the paraphrased words of the tentmaker of Tarsus, Paul, in his salutation to the community of early believers in Philippi: "May our God, who has begun a good work in you, bring it to completion [perfection]" as you continue to minister to those in mourning, standing as Christ's visible and tangible presence among them and giving them a renewed sense of hope and understanding.

CHAPTER 27

Wake Up, All You Preachers!

Wake up all you preachers [teachers], time to teach a new way.

Maybe, then they'll listen to what you have to say.

— Harold Melvin and the Blue Notes, "Wake Up Everybody"

The task of creating a new paradigm for understanding life after death and where the souls of the dearly departed end up going weighs heavily upon those charged with ministering to the bereaved, namely, preachers, teachers, and catechists. While most would agree that Heaven is not a physical place but a state of spiritual habitation, the language, symbolism, and imagery employed in speaking about Heaven often convey a sense that those who have died are going to a place far beyond our reach to become inhabitants of a celestial world. Nothing could be further from the truth!

How did the notion of "going up yonder" become indelibly etched in the minds of so many believers? A large swath of teachers and preachers have developed their concept or image of Heaven based upon or inspired by a vision, not reality, that the apostle John had while exiled on the island of Patmos as well as upon the biblical pronouncement of Jesus in John 14:2 of "many mansions in my Father's house." Such images as Heaven with twelve entrance gates and with walls of jasper and streets of purest gold confuse the mind and transmit false images as to the nature of Heaven. Images of a throne encircled by angels and saints wearing halos and bedecked in long white robes and golden slippers have colored most Christians' views of the Afterlife.

For most Christians, Heaven is a final destination where the spirits of the deceased go after an earthly life to inherit an eternal house "not built by human hands" (2 Cor. 5:1/NAB) and to partake in an eternal banquet. Never mind that the apostle Paul reminded the believer that "flesh and blood [the things pertaining to physical life] cannot inherit the kingdom of God" (1 Cor. 15:50/NAB). Nonetheless, there are still those who cling to the notion that Heaven has to be "a place" far beyond our reach or accessibility.

The daunting challenge that the presenters of the Word face today in contemporary society is proclaiming a faithful rendition of the Scriptures as it relates to death and the Afterlife. They can ill afford to sit back on their laurels by parroting what has been taught traditionally without thorough scrutiny. They must commit themselves to doing the necessary scholarly research, study, critical analysis, and biblical exegesis about Heaven and hell and juxtapose the result with what has been traditionally and habitually trumpeted about the heavenly realm.

There can be no excuse whatsoever for taking a lackadaisical approach to teaching believers about an issue that is most critical to them. How does that which is mortal take on immortality and that which is corruptible take on incorruptibility (1 Cor. 15:50), yet not need a material or physical place to exist? The onus rests squarely upon the shoulders of those who have been called and chosen by God to serve as the bridge between Earth and eternity. The people of God have been fed pablum for far too long regarding the mythical places called *Heaven* and *hell*. They need to have the milk bottle removed and replaced with the meat, namely, with the truth, the whole truth, and nothing but the truth.

As pastors, prophets, and catechists, we need to arrive at a point where we can address the masses of believers as spiritual people, not as infants. Even the apostle Paul faced a similar dilemma when ministering to the early believers in Corinth: "Indeed, you are still not able, even now, for you are still of the flesh" (1 Cor. 3:1–2/NAB).

As ministers of the Book and the Cup, we have been indulging our adherents on a steady diet of milk, not solid food, because we felt that they were unable to embrace an understanding of Heaven as what it truly is — returning to the Source from whence we came and dwelling in the fullness of God's nature and Essence. Instead of trying to scare the hell "into" them, we should teach them the truth that there is no such place as hell as has been traditionally taught. The real hell resides in our midst and can inhabit any of us. Our responsibility as shepherds is to teach people how to resist in faith the powers of darkness and evil so that the enemy will flee (1 Pet. 5:9)!

Preachers, as was trumpeted by famed attorney Johnnie Cochran in the O. J. Simpson trial: "If it doesn't fit, you must acquit." What has been taught and preached for centuries about Heaven and hell simply does not fit. It is time to jettison the myths. It is time to preach and teach the truth! Maybe, just maybe, they will then listen to what we preachers have to say!

Wake up, all you preachers!

CHAPTER 28

A Paradigm Shift in the Way
We Sing and Express Sympathy

We gather together as family members, relatives, and friends to commemorate and celebrate the life, love, and legacy of a dearly departed loved one by engaging in the ritual of a funeral or homegoing service. Our expressions of sympathy and condolence take the form of prayers, readings, songs, flowers, proclamations, and sympathy cards.

Music plays a very integral role in consoling and comforting those left behind. The lyrics contained therein are meant to soothe, release the emotional pressure valve, and reassure the attendees that their loved one is at peace. Words also express the community's belief and understanding of the reality of death. Oftentimes, the lyrics are not biblically rooted or catechetically connected. They lack theological depth and thus provide a false impression of what occurs to the soul after death in regard to the spirit's return to the Source.

A number of so-called Negro spirituals that surfaced during the slavery period are the main culprit! The lyrics to many of the songs were heavily influenced by Slave narratives, with the slaveowners' explicit intention of convincing slaves they need not be preoccupied with seeking Heaven on

Earth but should look forward to inheriting comfort in the next life, after death. It was a psychological control tactic, to say the least, to keep Black folks in submission and subservient to their masters! Such songs as "In the Sweet By and By," "Deep River," "I'll Fly Away," "Steal Away to Jesus," "Goin' Up Yonder," "Swing Low, Sweet Chariot," and "I Shall Wear a Crown," just to name a few, were all designed to convey to the naïve slave the false notion that their experience of Heaven on Earth could wait! Slave songs helped spread and impress the narrative. Those songs are still being currently heralded in a lot of traditional and fundamentalist Black Christian churches.

A serious examination of the lyrical content in ecclesiastic hymnology related to life after death will quickly reveal that there is a paucity of hymns and songs that speak directly to the true meaning of eternal life. Many composers of sacred music have not undergone the rigors of in-depth biblical and theological studies to bring forth the richness of an authentic expression of life after death in their lyrical renditions. For example, how many hymns or songs sung at a funeral, Mass of Christian Burial, or homegoing service speak of the spirit returning unto God who gave it, or God and Heaven being one and the same or, furthermore, about the intimate and inseparable relationship between God and those who have returned unto God? Are there any hymns that speak of possessing the fullness of the divine traits, characteristics, and attributes that exist in God? What about Heaven not being a place with material properties but a state of spiritual existence where the soul wants for nothing?

A paradigm shift is desperately needed in developing hymns and songs that are aligned with scriptural texts that correctly speak of life after death. If the lyrics are not biblically and theologically sound, they will continue to create and heap false notions and concepts of the Afterlife upon the believer. It is no wonder that so many Christians believe that after death they are going to live in a city in the sky with twelve gates, built with walls of jasper and streets of purest gold, while wearing golden slippers and long white robes and waving palm branches! If they hear and sing the same old songs repeatedly that reinforce these concepts, then one should not be surprised as to what will follow.

Attempting to convince a believer who has held on to inaccurate presentations and teachings about life after death is more than a notion. It is a gargantuan task that requires Herculean strength! Anyone attempting to undo age-old myths about a place called *Heaven* — with a throne, altar, angels, trumpets, banquets halls, and God sitting in judgment — is greeted with suspicion and disbelief. Folks would rather cling to these antiquated, old-fashioned, visionary concepts than jettison such falsities for the truth as contained in the Word of God.

The same paradigm shift applies to those individuals, organizations, and companies engaged in the creation of sympathy and condolence cards. A lot of the messages contained in the cards sound sweet, tender, and comforting but are not biblically correct, such as "God saw how much your loved one was suffering and gently called him/her home." God does not call anyone, good or bad, from living life on Earth to eternal life. God only steps in after a person has died and receives the spirit of God that resided in that individual back into the fullness of the Godhead.

A lucrative business enterprise awaits those who will undertake the tedious and demanding process of composing sympathy and condolence cards that properly reflect and relate to life after death from a biblical perspective as stated above.

It is high time for a paradigm shift in the way we sing and express sympathy that will convey the true meaning of what we believe, not what we imagine!

CHAPTER 29

Meditation on a Cemetery, Urn, and Obituary

Every now and then, each of our lives intersects with signs and symbols that remind us of the mortality and feebleness of human life. For some, these occurrences present themselves more often than one would expect. As a pastor who has officiated at hundreds of funerals or homegoing services for almost half a century, I am engaged in a daily meditation about the profound meaning of life and death. Most of those moments are a result of sentiments stirred up by seeing a cemetery or an urn or reading a newspaper obituary.

If you have ever taken a ride on Amtrak's Northeast Regional train from Washington, DC, to New York City, one cannot help but notice a proliferation of cemeteries dotting the landscape along the western stretch of the railroad tracks. There must have been a concerted effort by city and rural planners to place burial grounds so close to a mode of transportation. Perhaps it was a sly attempt to provide easy access to resurrected souls on the train to glory!

Recently, while driving alone along a pastoral stretch of road in Delaware, I found myself meditating upon the many tombstones in a cemetery.

What immediately came to mind was a joke I often use to spoof others, especially my two sons: "I wonder how many people are dead in that cemetery?" Of course, the answer is, "All of them!" Reminiscing, I quickly moved on to a more serious contemplation. One day, I, too, will lie among the dead and others will pass by the cemetery and ponder, "There he lies in state." In one sense, it's a morbid thought, realizing that a cemetery is the final resting place for our earthly "tent," as the apostle Paul referred to the body. In another sense, it is a stark reality that one day death will befall all of us.

Perhaps, it's the thought of one day lying in the earth, as if one would be experiencing the cold, damp, decomposing nature of one's body being consumed by worms and maggots, that most disturbs us. But how will it, since we will be dead?

For many of us, most of our earthly life is behind us, not before us! We are closer to being buried in a cemetery or having our skeletal remains placed in an urn. Soon and very soon, we will not be reading the newspaper obituary about the passing of others but having our own photo and name placed in such a column and being read and viewed by someone else! I cannot tell you how many times I have said when greeted by another with the words, "It's so great to see you," that I have retorted, "It's better to be seen than to be viewed!" It always brings a smile and chuckle from others when hearing it, but it serves as a sober reminder that there will come a time when each of us will lie in state. The grave still awaits!

A meditation on a cemetery, urn, and obituary just might be the remedy we need to live life to the fullest while we can still be seen and not viewed! When our physical lives have ebbed away, there will be no repeat performances! So, go for the gold, NOW!

CHAPTER 30

Our Father, Who Art in Thyself

The "Our Father" or "Lord's Prayer" is the singularly most mentioned and uttered prayer in all of Christianity. It is a universal prayer expressed by every Christian denomination within the Body of Christ and is often the first prayer formula memorized by those embracing the faith. The only substantive variance is at its conclusion, where some traditions add, "For Thine is the kingdom, the power, and the glory forever." Otherwise, it is the same, except for slight modifications due to whatever version of the Bible is used:

> Our Father, who art in Heaven,
> Hallowed be Thy Name.
> Thy Kingdom come.
> Thy will be done
> On earth as it is in Heaven.
> Give us this day our daily bread,
> And forgive us our trespasses,
> As we forgive those who trespass against us.
> And lead us not into temptation,
> But deliver us from evil.
> For Thine is the kingdom, the power, and the glory forever.
> AMEN.

How many times has this prayer been recited and offered to God, our Creator and Heavenly Parent, without ever thinking or considering "Our Father" and "Heaven" as one and the same? God is Heaven and Heaven is God! They are not two separate and distinct Entities. God does not reside in Heaven; Heaven resides in God and IS God. For God to be confined to a place called *Heaven,* as most of us have been taught to envision, would restrict and limit God's ubiquitous or omnipresent nature.

We can bring ourselves to a deeper understanding of this universal prayer if we look at it from a different angle or perspective that is in divine alignment with the premise and thesis contained in this book. Consider and meditate upon this novel version of the Lord's Prayer in the context of God and Heaven as one and the same Entity:

Our Father who art in [Thyself] Heaven,

Hallowed be Thy Name.

Thy Kingdom [of Thy manifest presence] come [within us].

Thy will be done

On Earth [in those made of clay] as it is in Heaven [Thee].

Give us this day our daily bread [all that we need to

become one as Thee],

And forgive us our trespasses [to the extent] as we forgive those

who trespass against us.

And lead us not into temptation [so that we may not be subjected

to the test],

But deliver us from evil [because no evil can dwell in Thee or those

who are within Thee].

For Thine is the Kingdom [the Kingdom and Thou art one and
the same], the power [Thou can doeth all things], and the glory
[Thou art praise] forever.
AMEN.

Once we reach the point in our spiritual growth and development where we view God and Heaven as one, we will understand that our ultimate quest is to become everything that God is in the same manner and form that Jesus, the Christ, our Elder Brother who became Lord and Savior, achieved in his earthly life (Heb. 5:7–9). Then we, too, shall one day be like Jesus, who became "God made man." Until that moment arrives for each of us, let us embody the words of Saint Augustine of Hippo: "Our souls are restless, Oh God, until they rest in Thee," for Thou art Heaven and Heaven is Thee.

CHAPTER 31

No Regrets!

Live your earthly life in such a way that when the hour of death comes you will have no regrets! Make your mark on the world by living each day to the fullest, as if it were your first day, your last day, your only day! In that way, when your individual life ceases to exist as you know it, the good you've done will not "be interred with [your] bones" (Mark Antony in the play Julius Caesar). It was the French writer François Mauriac who said, "No love, no friendship can cross the path of our destiny without leaving some mark on it forever." When you make an indelible mark upon the lives of others, you continue to live through them even after your physical demise.

Therefore, seek fulfillment NOW; love and reconcile with family, relatives, and friends; and do your best to leave no stone unturned and no task unfinished! As the expression goes, *"Tomorrow is promised to no one."* In the words of a great Catholic saint, Teresa of the Infant Jesus, *"I will spend my Heaven doing good upon Earth."* Likewise, when the inevitable moment arrives, you will have no regrets as to what awaits you beyond the grave or the crematorium.

Perhaps the reason why so many of us either fear death or cannot adjust to its reality is because of the uncertainties it holds, the first being: How can

I be sure there is life after death? What will it be like, or will I know that it is real? Will I be with my loved ones who have preceded me in death, and will I recognize and be reunited with them for all eternity, never again having to die or want for anything? But what if it is not so, and I simply fade away into nonexistence? Well, if there is no life in the Great Beyond, then there is absolutely nothing with which to be preoccupied. We will simply "be" in oblivion! However, better to live and die with the belief that eternal life exists rather than live and die with no hope.

There are many nagging concerns that make death both unanticipated and undesirable, especially feelings of helplessness, loss, or total uncontrol over that final moment. Some wonder if there will be any sense of consciousness to even know we have died. What will it be like? Will it be an experience of being swept away in a vortex of overwhelming and intense light, as those with near-death experiences have conveyed? Or will we tremble in fear as our earthly thoughts and deeds are revealed and exposed before the judgment seat of God?

Are we afraid of death because we are still unsure as to whether we will merit Heaven or be sentenced to eternal damnation in hell, no matter how holy we are or how strong is our faith? Let's admit it: The institutional church has done such a hell of a job brainwashing its constituents that most of us will still be wondering on our deathbeds if we have done enough good to inherit eternal life!

How does a person live a healthy life in such a way so as not to be intimidated or captivated by the grip of death? It begins with the recognition and acceptance of the undeniable fact that every person born of the flesh is going to physically die, no matter how unpleasant and unimaginable that may seem, especially when it relates to self. As the saying may be paraphrased, "You can run from death but you cannot hide!" The Book of

Ecclesiastes makes it plain: *"There is a time and season for every purpose under the heavens; a time to be born and a time to die" (3:1/NAB)*. We are going to die just as surely as we were born!

There are countless choices we make in life. However, there are two "choices" we never need to worry about: how we are born and when we will die. If our physical lives are finite, temporal, and transitory, then we should make every effort to view them within the spiritual context of that which is infinite, eternal, and incorruptible. When we come to a spiritual awareness that we are essentially spirit beings robed in flesh, we do not fear the disrobing of the body from the spirit based upon the firm belief that "to be absent from the body is to be present with the Lord" (2 Cor. 5:8/ KJV). Life is measured and contained in the essence of the divine presence housed within our mortal frames. There is great comfort and reassurance in the Word of God:

> Then man's dust will go back to the earth, returning to what it was, and the spirit will return to the God who gave it (Eccles. 12:7/ ISV).

Let's unpack this mystery of faith as rooted in Genesis and expounded throughout the Scriptures. If the Word of God is true (and I wholeheartedly and without reservation believe it to be so), each one of us was created in the divine image and likeness of our Creator (Gen. 1:26), who is absolute, unique, unchanging, and eternal. If God has no beginning and no end, then that which bears God's spiritual DNA contains the same essence as its Creator. Although we did not have a conscious awareness or knowledge of that spiritual existence while being embedded in the very nature of God, the all-knowing God did! The prophet Jeremiah, confronted with his own identity and calling, was overwhelmed by the magnitude of his divine mission. God comforted and reassured him: *"Before I formed thee in the belly, I knew thee"* (*Jer. 1:5/KJV*). If Jeremiah had no existence prior to being conceived in the womb of his mother, then how could his existence have been known?

We often equate life itself within the context of physical existence. Yet, the breath that sustains us is the spiritual essence of God dwelling within our corporeal temples (1 Cor. 3:16). Without breath, life ceases to exist. No breath, no life! Ask the prophet Ezekiel (chapter 37) if it ain't so! While the body lies in the sleep of death, the spirit that was the engine lives on and returns to become a part of the Essence from whence it came. There is life beyond the flesh that continues to manifest itself in omnipotent, omniscient, and omnipresent ways in the same manner as its Progenitor. Wherever God is, so are the ones who have spiritually ascended and have been reunited with "the ground of their being," in the words of Paul Tillich. They return unto God and are embedded in or engrafted to the fullness of God and become one and the same as God.

While on Earth, they were identified by their biologically given name. When they died, they returned to God and embraced their original name, as it was in the beginning. Their eternal name becomes *God*! If man and woman came forth from the oneness of God and had no other identity or name than that of *God* before they came forth from their mother's womb, then why would they not be known by that same name when returning unto its Essence?

The challenge for the believer is coming to a deep understanding of the nature of God — how God exists and functions in a manner that goes far beyond what the human mind can grasp or imagine. It all boils down to whether we trust in God's Word and believe within the depths of our hearts that God has prepared a better place for us (Heb. 11:16 and John 14:3). The human mind cannot even begin to grasp that which is beyond the physical dimensions of life. So, stop trying! Take it to God in prayer.

God's ways are inscrutable! Just as the Lord's thoughts are above our thoughts and God's ways above our ways (Isa. 55:9), any attempt by the human mind to penetrate or unravel the mysterious ways or nature of God borders on an exercise in futility! Let God be God and allow God to handle the situation when death comes for each of us. For if we die and there is no life after death, then God, too, is dead! But God is not dead. God is still alive!

Believe God and trust Him at His Word! After all, what is left when all else is gone? Jesus said, "But be of good cheer; I have overcome the world" (John 16:33/KJV). As a believer you, too, can overcome the world by having no fear of death or its deceptive power over you.

When that hour comes, let there be no regrets!

CHAPTER 32

The Final Word

"When the perishable has been clothed with the imperishable, and the mortal with immortality, then the saying that is written will come true: 'Death has been swallowed up in victory. Where, O death, is your victory? Where, O death, is your sting?'" (1 Cor. 15:54–55/NIV).

When I think of death, the first thing that comes to mind is "F.E.A.R.," that is: "False Evidence Appearing Real." Fear can subject us to lifelong spiritual slavery that prevents us from accessing the freedom inherent in being divinely created as children of God. The Book of Hebrews cries out, "And free those who through fear of death had been subject to slavery all their life" (2:15/NIV). If we are enslaved by false things that appear as real but are only mere shadows of our doubts and anxieties — "Yea, though I walk through the valley of the shadow of death I fear no evil" (Ps. 23:4a/ KJV) — we cannot realize and actualize our greatness as well as achieve our destiny in life. We must constantly remind ourselves that we have been "fearfully and wonderfully made" by God (Ps. 139:14/NIV).

We fear the unknown, the uncertain, and that which appears to be above and beyond our power or control. Questions plague us, such as, what will happen to us after we physically die?; will we make it to Heaven?; will we miss the mark and be tormented in hell for all eternity?; will we see and remain forever with our loved ones who have preceded us in death?; what will life be like in the Great Beyond?; is the final resting place a physical or spiritual dwelling?; and last, but certainly not least, after we physically die will we possess a consciousness of life beyond the grave or will memory permanently cease to exist?

All these probing questions instill fear in practically everyone, even as we aspire to place trust in God and find solace in His holy Word. Certainly, there are moments when each of us doubts if the end of life will be more than what we could ever imagine or dream of. Could it be that God has something better in store for us (Heb. 11:40) that "eye hath not seen, nor ear heard, neither have entered into the heart of man, the things which God hath prepared for them that love Him" (1 Cor. 2:9/KJV)?

Fear can erase or contaminate God's ultimate plan in our mind if our preoccupation with physical life trumps our walk by faith (2 Cor. 5:7). Every day is a test of our faith! Circumstances and situations can arise and discombobulate us to such an extent that we question even the very existence of God as well as if God really cares or is concerned about our welfare. The downside of life allows negativity and inharmonious vibrations to creep in through the crevices of our mind and sow seeds of doubt about the very nature of human existence itself. After all, life is no "crystal stair" (Langston Hughes, "Mother to Son")! It has its moments when we even begin to doubt ourselves!

The way to conquer the fear of death is to admit, first and foremost, that death is part and parcel of living. There is a time and season for every purpose under the heavens, a time to be born and a time to die (Eccles. 3:2). As troubling as it may seem to most of us, we are all going to die! There is nowhere to run and nowhere to hide. If we know that we are going to physically die, it might help if we lived by the philosophy of the ancient

Egyptians: "We live to die!" For them, death was not the end of life but only a transition to another plane of reality.

Yet, we still fear death! But what does the Word of God tell us about death? Can we find reassurance while seeking a more abundant life (John 10:10) so that death will not ultimately claim victory over us?

First of all, the Word of God boldly proclaims that death has no sting and it has no victory (1 Cor. 15:55). Even though we all must experience physical death, it possesses no power over us. If anything, death is a release valve that removes the pressure of the demands of everyday living and allows the spirit to escape! There is a reason why we use the expression *expire* to refer to the time of death. *Ex* is the Latin prefix for *exit* or *out*, and *spire* comes from the Latin verb *spirare*, which means *breath*. So, when a person expires the breath goes out! And the only way for that to happen is if that which "goes out" is alive and active!

The profound mystery of life, in and of itself, is rooted in God's spectacular creation of man and woman as a composite of both spirit and flesh. The Spirit of the Invisible God is blown into mortal flesh and makes it live, move, and have its being. Man and woman thus become living souls or beings. The duality of their nature is both eternal and temporal, immortal and mortal, incorruptible and corruptible. One's spiritual nature informs and transforms one's physical nature to a higher degree of understanding and relativity. Coming to an acceptance of such a belief helps us to view the fullness of life as eternal!

"Behold, I tell you a mystery. We shall not all fall asleep, but we will all be changed, in an instant, in the blink of an eye, at the last trumpet. For the trumpet will sound, the dead will be raised incorruptible, and we shall be changed. For that which is corruptible must clothe itself with incorruptibility, and that which is mortal must clothe itself with immortality. And when this which is corruptible clothes itself with incorruptibility and this which is mortal clothes itself with immortality, then the word that is written shall come about: 'Death is swallowed up in victory'" (1 Cor. 15:51–54/NIV).

The Word of God reminds us that we were made from the dust of the Earth and unto that same dust we shall return (Gen. 3:19). Yet, it was into that dust that God breathed the breath of life (spirit), and man and woman became living beings/souls (Gen. 2:7). In the final analysis, there is a time and season for every purpose, a time to be born and a time to die (Eccles. 3:1–2).

The breath or spirit is from the very Essence or nature of God. The flesh is of the Earth. The troubling words of the psalmist hit home: "When you [God] hide your face, they are lost. When you take away their breath, they perish and return to the dust from which they came. When you send forth your breath, they are created; and you renew the face of the earth" (Ps. 104:29–30/NIV).

The Book of Ecclesiastes 12:7 further elucidates the point: "And the dust returns to the earth as it once was, and the life breath returns to God who gave it." One of the apocryphal writings has a similar declaration: "All that is of earth returns to earth, and what is from above returns above" (Sir. 40:11).

But, thanks be to God, death will ultimately be destroyed forever and have no sway over us (Isa. 25:8)! The Bible reassures us that the day of death is better than the day of birth (Eccles. 7:1)! Death is nothing more and nothing less than a portal that places us on a path to eternal life. For many believers, that path leads to Heaven, which begs the questions: Where is Heaven, who is there, and what does it look like?

AS IT WAS IN THE BEGINNING.....

The ultimate goal of human life is to return to the Source from which we came.

So, what is there to fear in releasing our mortal frame back to the dust from whence it came if it means living with and in God for eternity? If we have confidence and trust in God's Word when the hour of inevitability comes, we can rest assured, knowing that we have "nothing to fear but F.E.A.R. itself" (Franklin Delano Roosevelt).

Jesus, the Christ, said it best: "Don't be afraid. I am here!" (John 6:20/NLT). In the end, the Word of God will have the final word!

Sample Letter to the Bereaved at a Time of Loss

November 17, 2022

To the Beloved Family of the late_____:
Peace be with you! On behalf of the entire Faith Community of
_____, we wish to express our undying love, support,
and unity with you as you gather for the (Funeral/Mass of Christian Burial/
Homegoing Service/Seonghwa) to honor, remember, and celebrate the life
of your dearly departed loved one,_____.

Words seem so inadequate in comforting those who have lost a loved
one or reassuring them that everything will be all right "in the sweet by and
by." No kind gesture or expression of love in the hour of death can heal the
wounded spirit, fill the vacuum that one experiences, or remove a sense of
emptiness at the time of physical separation from someone who has left
an indelible mark upon our hearts. "No love, no friendship can ever cross
the path of our destiny without leaving some mark on it forever" (François
Mauriac).

We who believe in God as Creator and Heavenly Parent and in Jesus,
the Christ, as the Resurrection and the Life as well as our Elder Brother,

cling to the tenets of our Faith, which teach us that, in death, life is changed, not ended. The Word of God reminds us that "the dust shall return to the earth as it once was, and the life breath [spirit] shall return to God who gave it" (Ecclesiastes 12:7). The eternal breath that sustained God's Life in _____ at the moment of physical conception in his (her) mother _____'s womb has returned unto God and remains alive and present wherever God dwells. God and he (she) are now One, and the pangs of death shall no longer have any claim over her (him). She (he) is free from all of her (his) earthly labors and now lives with God forevermore. That which made your loved one, _____, "live and move and have her (his) being" (Acts 17:28) is now "absent from the body and is present with the Lord" (2 Corinthians 5:8).

Let these consoling words of one of the greatest doctors and teachers in Christianity be your guiding light as you probe the mystery of death: "Those whom we have loved and lost are no longer where they were before. They are now wherever we are" (Saint John Chrysostom). If God is ever present with us here on Earth, then so are our loved ones who are eternally present in God.

When your heart is sad and weary and you feel like you just can't keep on keeping on in the throes of physical loss, just look for God, and there you will find _____ having the time of her (his) life and waiting for your glorious return to the Source to be one with her (him) and God.

"Let not your heart be troubled" (John 14:1).

In the Peace of the Risen Christ,

Name of Pastor/Minister

Title and Church

Group Discussion

Background Information

Beyond the Zoom: The Afterlife offers a new paradigm for viewing death and life after death by removing the "sting of death" that is often associated with mortal transition. It presents the essence of life, namely, the spirit, as eternal and its temporary housing in the body as transient, referred to as the Zoom Effect. Once the spirit of God that dwells in everyone created in the "image and likeness of God" (Gen. 1:26) exits the body, it "returns unto the Source from which it came" (Eccles. 12:7b).

The book examines and scrutinizes, in the light of the Word of God, topics such as the Afterlife in mythology and religion; Heaven, hell, and purgatory; questions regarding recognizing our loved ones after we die; communicating with spirits; and where the spirit or soul goes after it exits the body. As all of us came from the oneness of God, so shall we return to become one with God in all things.

Many readers will find affirmation regarding beliefs they have privately held and treasured all their lives about life after death. Some will be dumbfounded, as a result of having been reared and catechized in the cauldrons of fundamental and traditional teachings on the Afterlife, causing them to attack the book's premises without proof to the contrary.

Where the reader stands on the issues of death and the Afterlife often depends on how a person has been catechized or raised in one's particular faith expression. Other important factors relate to one's family background; religious, national, or ethnic traditions; one's level of indoctrination; and the consistency with which the church, temple, synagogue, or mosque has honed the subjects for centuries.

The Group Discussion

While it is virtually impossible to have a *tabula rasa*, or a "mind not yet affected by experiences or expressions," in the reading and discussion of *Beyond the Zoom: The Afterlife*, you are invited to take "The Faith Challenge." The process consists of asking both believers and nonbelievers to share in a group setting their understanding of death and the Afterlife. The smaller the gathering, the better. In that way, everyone gets a chance to speak his or her mind by honestly sharing their viewpoints and hearing those of others.

"The Faith Challenge"

Following are some suggested questions to stimulate discussion and dialogue. Please feel free to add your own. Each group should select a facilitator to maintain order and to allow everyone to present their views. It is important to remember that everyone has a right to present and share their faith, opinions, and understanding without fear of prejudice or condemnation.

Suggested Questions for Discussion

- How does your understanding of the Afterlife correlate or resonate with what you have read in the book?

- What new and challenging approach or understanding to the subject of death and the Afterlife did it present?

- What in the book differed most from your cherished beliefs?

- After reading the book, what, if anything, has changed or needs to be altered in how you view death and the Afterlife?

- After juxtaposing your understanding of death and the Afterlife with what you have read in the book, can there be an assimilation with your currently held beliefs that will give you a better understanding of death and the Afterlife?

- How has the book challenged your current understanding? How has it changed your thinking or opinion?

- What are the "non-negotiables" when it comes to your beliefs about death and the Afterlife?

- After reading the book, does it make you less or more afraid to die? State a couple of examples of how the book aided you in facing the reality of death without fear.

- Do you believe that Heaven is a physical place with "mansions, walls of jasper, and streets of purest gold" or that it is a state of spiritual existence? Explain your choice and how you came to that conclusion.

- Can you embrace the book's viewpoint or statement that hell is not a physical place of "fire and brimstone" where there is the "wailing and gnashing of teeth" — that hell is, rather, right here on Earth? If not, why not?

- Does it trouble you that even bad or the worst people in life can be redeemed and ultimately return unto the Source from which they came? Cite an example from the book that clarifies why and how it can happen.

- What does it mean to say that "God is Heaven and Heaven is God"? How does the book reach such a conclusion?

- Do you believe that it is possible to communicate with the dead, or do you consider such an act voodoo? How does the book state that it is possible?

Please feel free to add additional questions.

Another option: Take one chapter at a time, read it together, and then open the floor for discussion.

Thank you for your participation.

Printed in the USA
CPSIA information can be obtained
at www.ICGtesting.com
LVHW060005031023
759781LV00108B/3539